iCONLOGiC™

Version: 072119
Page Count: 264
ISBN's:
9781944607487 (Perfect-Bound Print Book)
9781944607494 (Coil-Bound Print Book & PDF)
9781944607500 (eBook)

Adobe Captivate 2019:
The Essentials (Second Edition)

"Skills and Drills" Learning

Kevin Siegel

Official

IconLogic Certified Adobe Captivate Developer

courseware

IconLogic Certified
Adobe Captivate
Developer

ICACD

Cp

Get certified from the people who **literally**
wrote the book on Adobe Captivate

https://www.iconlogic.com/instructor-led-training/certifications.html

iCONLOGiC
"Skills and Drills" Learning

Contents

NOTES

NOTES

NOTES

Notes

iCONLOGiC
"Skills and Drills" Learning

About This Book

This Section Contains Information About:

- The Author, page viii
- About IconLogic, page viii
- Confidence Checks, page ix
- Software & Asset Requirements, page ix
- Data Files (Captivate Project Assets), page ix
- How Software Updates Affect This Book, page xi
- Contacting IconLogic, page xi

NOTES

The Author

Kevin Siegel is the founder and president of IconLogic, Inc. He has written hundreds of step-by-step computer training books on applications such as *Adobe Captivate, Articulate Storyline, Adobe RoboHelp, Adobe Presenter, Adobe Technical Communication Suite, Adobe Dreamweaver, Adobe InDesign, Microsoft Office, Microsoft PowerPoint, QuarkXPress,* and *TechSmith Camtasia.*

Kevin spent five years in the U.S. Coast Guard as an award-winning photojournalist and has three decades' experience as a print publisher, technical writer, instructional designer, and eLearning developer. He is a certified technical trainer, a veteran classroom instructor, and a frequent speaker at trade shows and conventions. Kevin holds multiple certifications from Adobe and CompTIA. He is also a Certified Online Training Professional (COTP) with the International Council for Certified Online Training Professionals (ICCOTP). You can reach Kevin at **ksiegel@iconlogic.com**.

About IconLogic

Founded in 1992, IconLogic is a training, eLearning development, and publishing company offering services to clients across the globe.

As a training company, IconLogic has directly trained thousands of professionals both onsite and online on dozens of applications. As a publishing company, IconLogic has published hundreds of critically-acclaimed books and created technical documents for both print and digital publication. And as a development company, IconLogic has produced content for some of the largest companies in the world including, but not limited to, ADP, ADT, The World Bank, Heineken, EverFi, Bank of America, Fresenius Kabi, FAA, Wells Fargo, American Express, Microsoft, Department of For-Hire Vehicles, Federal Reserve Bank of Richmond, Coast Guard, Marine Corps, Canadian Blood, Canadian Natural Resources, DC Child and Family Services, and the Department of Defense. You can learn more about IconLogic's varied services at www.iconlogic.com.

Book Conventions

Learners learn best by doing, not just by watching or listening. With that simple concept in mind, IconLogic books are created by trainers and/or authors with years of experience training adult learners. Each IconLogic book contains a minimal amount of text and is loaded with hands-on activities, screen captures, and challenge exercises to reinforce newly acquired skills.

This book has been divided into several modules. Because each module builds on lessons learned in a previous module, it is recommended that you complete each module in succession.

Here is the lesson key:

❏ instructions for you to follow look like this (the boxes are also used in bulleted lists)

If you are expected to type anything or if something is important, it is set in bold type like this:

❏ type **9** into the text area

If you are expected to press a key on your keyboard, the instruction looks like this:

❏ press [**shift**]

If you have any comments or questions about this book or any IconLogic services, please see the last page of this section for IconLogic's contact information.

Confidence Checks

As you move through the lessons in this book, you will come across the little guy at the right. He indicates a Confidence Check. Throughout each module, you are guided through hands-on, step-by-step exercises. But at some point you'll have to fend for yourself. That is where Confidence Checks come in. Please be sure to complete each of the challenges because some exercises build on completed Confidence Checks.

Software & Asset Requirements

To complete the lessons presented in this book, you will need Adobe Captivate **version 2019 (11.5)** for the Mac or PC installed on your computer. Captivate does not come with this book but a free trial version can be downloaded from Adobe.com.

You will need to download this book's project assets (data files) that have been created specifically to support this book and this version of Captivate (See the "Data Files" section below).

You'll be hearing audio during some of the lessons so you'll either need a headset or speakers. And you'll be recording your own voiceover audio so you'll need some sort of microphone.

You will learn how to incorporate Microsoft PowerPoint presentations and Word documents into Captivate projects during this book. To complete those activities, you will need a recent version of PowerPoint and Word.

Data Files (Captivate Project Assets)

You're probably chomping at the bit, ready to dive into Captivate and begin creating eLearning lessons. Not so fast... do you have some sample projects? What about graphics? Do you have some sound effects to play with? No? No worries. I've got everything you need—I call them data files—and they can be downloaded from the IconLogic website for free.

Windows users: Work through the following activity.

Mac users: Skip the following activity and go to the Mac activity on page x.

Guided Activity: Download the Windows Data Files

1. Download the PC student data files necessary to use this book.

   ☐ use a web browser and go to **http://www.iconlogic.com/pc**

   ☐ click the **Captivate 2019: The Essentials (Version 11.5)** link

   A dialog box may open, asking if you want to Save or Open (or Run) the file. (On some computers and some browsers, the file simply downloads to your Downloads folder without question.)

2. Download/save the file to your computer. (After the file downloads, close the web browser.)

3. Extract (Unzip) the data package.

   ☐ find the **Captivate2019Data** file you just downloaded to your computer

   ☐ double-click the file to execute it (even though the file is an EXE file, it's not a program; it's an archive only containing zipped Captivate projects and assets)

☐ if you receive a **Security message**, click the **Run** button

The WinZip Self Extractor opens.

☐ confirm **C:** appears in the **Unzip to Folder** area (you can click **Browse** and change the **Unzip to folder** location if you are not able to install directly to your C drive)

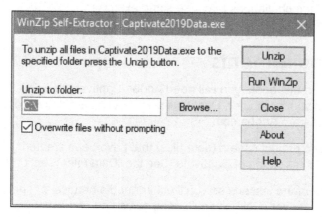

☐ click the **Unzip** button

Several files are unzipped.

☐ click the **OK** button and then click the **Close** button

The data files have been installed on your hard drive (within a folder named **Captivate2019Data**). As you move through the lessons in this book, you will be working with these files. You can skip the next activity and go to page xi.

Guided Activity: Download the Mac Data Files

1. Download the Mac student data files necessary to use this book.

    ☐ use a web browser and go to **http://www.iconlogic.com/mac**

    ☐ click the **Captivate 2019: The Essentials (Version 11.5)** link

    The zipped data files are typically downloaded to the **Downloads** folder on your Mac and are automatically extracted into the folder named **Captivate2019Data**.

2. Move the data files folder to your desktop.

    ☐ drag the **Captivate2019Data** folder from the **Downloads** folder to your desktop

3. You can now close the **Downloads** folder window and your web browser.

    Before starting the lessons in this book, it's a good idea to review "How Software Updates Affect This Book" on page xi.

How Software Updates Affect This Book

This book was written specifically to teach you how to use Adobe Captivate 2019. The Captivate version used for the creation of this book was **11.5.0.476**.

With each major release of Captivate, my intention is to write a new book to support that version and make it available within 30-60 days of the software being released by Adobe. From time to time, Adobe makes service releases/patches of Captivate available for customers that fix bugs or add functionality. For instance, I would expect Adobe to update Captivate with a patch or two within a few months of Captivate 2019 being released. That patched version might be called Captivate **11.5.01** or **11.5.1.1**. Usually these updates are minor (bug fixes) and have little or no impact on the lessons presented in this book. However, Adobe sometimes makes significant changes to the way Captivate looks or behaves, even with minor patches. (Such was the case when Adobe updated Captivate from version 5 to 5.5—about a dozen features were added, and a few panels were actually renamed, throwing readers of my books into a tizzy.)

Because it is not possible for me to recall and update printed books, some instructions you are asked to follow in this book may not match the patched/updated version of Captivate that you might be using. If something on your screen does not match what I am showing in the book, please visit the Adobe Captivate 2019 book product page on my website for possible updates (http://www.iconlogic.com/adobe-captivate-2019-essentials-workbook.html).

Contacting IconLogic

IconLogic, Inc.
Phone: 410.956.4949
Web: **www.iconlogic.com**
Email: **ksiegel@iconlogic.com**

Notes

iCONLOGiC

"Skills and Drills" Learning

Rank Your Skills

Before starting this book, complete the skills assessment on the next page.

Skills Assessment

How This Assessment Works

Below you will find 10 course objectives for *Adobe Captivate 2019: The Essentials (Second Edition)*. **Before starting the book:** Review each objective and rank your skills using the scale next to each objective. A rank of ① means **No Confidence** in the skill. A rank of ⑤ means **Total Confidence**. After you've completed this assessment, go through the entire book. **After finishing the book:** Review each objective and rank your skills now that you've completed the book. Most people see dramatic improvements in the second assessment after completing the lessons in this book.

Before-Class Skills Assessment

1. I can record a Software Simulation in Custom mode.	①	②	③	④	⑤
2. I can create a Quiz in Captivate.	①	②	③	④	⑤
3. I can insert a Text Caption.	①	②	③	④	⑤
4. I know how to use a Smart Shape as a Button.	①	②	③	④	⑤
5. I can insert Click Boxes.	①	②	③	④	⑤
6. I can use a Smart Shape as a Button.	①	②	③	④	⑤
7. I can add Text Entry Boxes.	①	②	③	④	⑤
8. I can create a TOC using the Skin Editor.	①	②	③	④	⑤
9. I can perform a "Round-trip" to Word.	①	②	③	④	⑤
10. I can publish as HTML5.	①	②	③	④	⑤

After-Class Skills Assessment

1. I can record a Software Simulation in Custom mode.	①	②	③	④	⑤
2. I can create a Quiz in Captivate.	①	②	③	④	⑤
3. I can insert a Text Caption.	①	②	③	④	⑤
4. I know how to use a Smart Shape as a Button.	①	②	③	④	⑤
5. I can insert Click Boxes.	①	②	③	④	⑤
6. I can use a Smart Shape as a Button.	①	②	③	④	⑤
7. I can add Text Entry Boxes.	①	②	③	④	⑤
8. I can create a TOC using the Skin Editor.	①	②	③	④	⑤
9. I can perform a "Round-trip" to Word.	①	②	③	④	⑤
10. I can publish as HTML5.	①	②	③	④	⑤

IconLogic, Inc.
"Skills and Drills" Learning
Web: www.iconlogic.com | Email: info@iconlogic.com

iCONLOGiC
"Skills and Drills" Learning

Preface

In This Module You Will Learn About:

Education Through Pictures

In a previous life, I was a professional photographer. When I wasn't snapping photos during a five-year tour with the U.S. Coast Guard, I covered media events in New York City as a freelance photographer.

Just about any photographer will tell you that the goal when taking pictures is to capture a story with a few, or maybe just one, photograph. I'm betting that you have heard the saying "a picture is worth a thousand words" more than once. As a professional photographer, I lived those words.

I have spent the bulk of my career attempting to perfect the art of teaching complex concepts to busy, distracted adult learners. I have always attempted to write documentation using as few words as possible and to teach lessons as efficiently as possible.

If you are in the business of educating, you know how difficult the job of writing relevant lesson plans with fewer and fewer words can be. My step-by-step workbooks have long been known for their "skills-and-drills learning" approach. The term "skills-and-drills" means different things to different people. For some, it means fast-moving lessons that do not drown a person with unnecessary information. For me, "skills-and-drills" means learning something by doing, whatever that something is. It also means learning with a heavy dose of visuals instead of a heavy dose of text.

I learned long ago that people tend to think not with words but with pictures. Here's an example of what I mean:

> Close your eyes for a second and picture **three** in your mind's eye.
>
> Open your eyes after a few seconds and read on.
>
> (See how precise I am? I know that some of you might have closed your eyes, kept them closed, and then fallen fast asleep without the last instruction.)

I wasn't specific when I asked you to picture **three** was I? Because I didn't tell you how to picture *three*, it's a good bet that things such as *three cupcakes, three bowls of ice cream,* or *three big boxes of Cap'n Crunch* (everyone knows that the Cap'n is the best breakfast cereal *ever*) flashed into your mind's eye. Maybe a large numeral 3 appeared in your mind's eye—not the word "three." In fact, I doubt that you visualized the word *three.* Why? As I said above, people tend to think in terms of images, not words. That's the reason most IconLogic books contain hundreds of screen captures and images that visually explain a concept that might have taken several paragraphs to explain. And when I do have to explain a concept, I make every effort to minimize the chatter and get right to the point.

Enough chatter... let's move on.

RoboDemo to Captivate

A picture can be nice, but it's static. No matter how good a picture is, it is limited in its ability to convey detailed information or concepts. Knowing this limitation, I searched for a program I could use to augment the activities presented in my books. I was specifically looking for a program that would make the lessons in my books come to life and allow me to create software simulations.

Over the years, I have used several programs that captured videos of my computer screen and mouse actions well enough, but the resulting videos were *huge*. A five-minute video can easily gobble up nearly 100 megabytes of storage space on a server. Downloading a file that large via the Internet can take a lot of time, even with a decent Internet connection.

Large file sizes were just one part of the problem. The output published by the early eLearning tools were not cross-platform (meaning that they would not work on both Macs and PCs running Windows). And the first eLearning lessons I created were simple videos that were not capable of being interactive. I firmly believe that *showing* something to learners isn't the same as *teaching* learners a skill and letting them actually *perform* the skill.

Early eLearning technology was so bad that I gave up on the idea and decided to wait until someone came up with a "killer" application. That program began life simply enough as a little utility called Flashcam (by Nexus Concepts, 2002). Flashcam was a simple screen capture application that made quick work of capturing just about anything you could do on your computer. Flashcam soon became the property of eHelp Software and was renamed RoboDemo. At that point, RoboDemo could be used to create sophisticated software demonstrations and interactive simulations.

eHelp Software was responsible for RoboDemo versions 3 through 5. After that, Macromedia (of Dreamweaver and Flash fame) acquired eHelp Software. Macromedia revamped RoboDemo, added even more awesome features, and changed the name of the program from RoboDemo to Captivate.

In 2005, Adobe Systems acquired Macromedia. Hence, the program has been known as *Adobe Captivate*. Adobe's first version of Captivate was Adobe Captivate 2.

If you're totally new to Adobe Captivate, the first thing you should consider is what the program can allow you to create. Microsoft Word is typically used to create standard text-based letters and documents. Adobe InDesign is typically used to create more visually-appealing, complex brochures, newspapers, and magazines. Adobe Acrobat is for creating PDFs. So what's up with Captivate? Using Adobe Captivate, you can create eLearning content about *anything*! Need to create an online lesson about onboarding? How about a course on conflict resolution? Perhaps a software simulation teaching colleagues how to attach a file to an email? You can use Captivate to create eLearning for all of these subjects and countless more.

The eLearning content you create with Captivate can be interactive—you can include text, images, clickable hotspots, quizzes, typing areas, sound effects, videos, special effects, voiceover audio, and more.

Finished Adobe Captivate projects can be published as Flash (SWF), HTML5, Word documents, PDFs, and MP4 videos. Learners can access your eLearning courses via a corporate web server, Learning Management System (LMS), or media server such as YouTube and Vimeo. And learners can use just about any kind of device to access your content including web browsers via desktop computers, laptops, and mobile devices such as smart phones and tablets.

Planning eLearning Projects

By the time you finish the last lesson, you should be able to use Captivate to create some compelling, technically sound eLearning lessons. However, publishing technically sound content does not necessarily mean creating *good* eLearning. If you want to create good, useful lessons, you have to plan ahead. Before creating a Captivate project, clarify the following:

❑ Why are you creating an eLearning course in the first place? You'd be surprised how many people start Captivate and just start creating content. This kind of development process might be well-intentioned, but you really need to map out the entire course, including how you are going to track learner comprehension (if that's important to you). During the mapping process, you might come to the conclusion that your course simply isn't appropriate for eLearning and move on to another course.

❑ Who is your audience? The way you teach children is different from the way you teach adults. For instance, children need praise and encouragement during the learning process that an adult learner might find annoying, if not down-right obnoxious.

❑ What exactly are you teaching, and is it appropriate for eLearning? Not every lesson in an instructor-led lesson can be effectively re-tooled as an eLearning lesson. For instance, if a course relies on breakout groups, group discussion, or collaborative work, those aspects of the course cannot be included in eLearning. Keep in mind that eLearners almost always work on their own with little or no interaction with a colleague.

❑ Does your project need to accommodate learners with disabilities? If the answer is yes, you should budget approximately 30 percent more time to produce each lesson. Although it's not difficult to create accessible eLearning, it takes time.

❑ Do you want your projects to contain images and background music? If so, where will you get them? Also, are you going to use a template? If so, who is going to design/create it?

❑ Will there be captions (written instructions and descriptions)? If so, who will write the content for these captions? Do you need an eLearning script? Do you need a voice-over script?

❑ Is your course soft-skills, or is it a software simulation? If it is soft-skills, does it make sense to create most of the content in Microsoft PowerPoint and then import the presentation into Captivate?

eLearning Development Phases

The infographic below offers a visual way to think about the eLearning development process and phases. A larger version of the graphic can be downloaded from www.iconlogic.com/skills-drills-workbooks/elearning-resources.html.

eLearning Development Phases

DISCOVERY

Meet with the client. Find out **what they want** in an ideal eLearning course. Who is the **audience**? Define a course **mission statement** for the course in general. You'll also need a mission statement for each lesson in the course. Will the course require **accessibility**? **Audio**? Will it need to be **localized**? What kind of **hardware** will students be using to access the course?

DESIGN

Which tool will you be using to develop the content (**Captivate, PowerPoint, Presenter, Storyline**, or perhaps a combination of a couple tools)? **Instructional design**, a **graphical treatment**, and **navigational choices** are now made and implemented.

WRITING and/or STORYBOARDING

Now that you have chosen a production tool and decided the overall design of the course, you'll need to **plot out the flow** of the course and **write a script and/or a storyboard**. If the course includes voiceover audio, you'll need a separate (and different) script for that.

PRODUCTION

Now it's time to get busy with the **development work** in the selected tool. This includes everything right up to the point of publishing. You'll also **beta test** the lessons in this phase as they are completed.

CLIENT APPROVAL

You're almost there! But, before project completion, you'll need to get your **client's approval**. Depending upon how this goes, **you may need to repeat parts of steps two, three, and four**.

PUBLISHING and IMPLEMENTATION

This includes not only **publishing locally**, but uploading the content to a **web server** or **LMS (SCORM or AICC)**. Be sure to allow time to work out bugs in this phase.

MAINTENANCE

You did a great job! But sometimes changes and updates are necessary. This phase includes **making updates** to the content and **re-posting to the LMS or web server**.

Brought to you by:
iCONLOGiC
www.iconlogic.com

NOTES

Budgeting Considerations

Many new eLearning developers underestimate the time needed to produce Captivate projects. Although it is certainly easier and faster to create eLearning content than ever before, it still takes time. To determine your level of effort, the first thing you need to know is how long you want your eLearning course to play (in minutes.) Once you have that number, you can calculate your level of effort.

Let's estimate how long it might to take to create a 60-minute eLearning course. Because you should not create a single Captivate project that, when published, plays for 60 consecutive minutes, it's ideal to break the 60 minutes of content into manageable chunks. I'd suggest that each chunk play for **no more than five minutes**. In that case, you will have 12 Captivate projects, each playing for five-minutes.

You need to design and then write the content for the course so you will need a script and/or storyboard. If there's going to be voice-over audio (I'd encourage you to include voice-over audio), you'll need a voice-over script.

Instructional Design includes the process of analyzing the course objectives and learner needs, writing mission statements, developing course success goals and mapping out a strategy for tracking the success or failure of the course.

Storyboards are rough sketches that show the general content of your project, slide by slide. If your projects contain more screen shots of an application than captions, a storyboard is a good idea.

Scripts are detailed step-by-step procedures. These are ideal if your project will contain a significant number of Text Captions.

Voice-over scripts are important because you don't want the narrator simply reading aloud the text displayed on the screen. Studies have shown that a narrator simply reading the text being displayed is a distraction to the learner.

It could take at least three hours to write a script to support a five-minute eLearning lesson. Therefore, you should budget at least 36 hours to write the entire one-hour eLearning course (12x3=36). Depending on how fast you write, you could easily double those hours, meaning you may need to budget approximately 80 hours for writing.

When creating content in Captivate, you can and should begin with a project template. A template is essentially a completed shell project that you will use as the basis of all of your projects. It's not difficult to create a template, but it takes time. An ideal template contains placeholders, an introduction slide, transitional slides, a conclusion slide, a skin, and appropriate Start and End Properties (although these terms may seem foreign to you now, you will learn about many of them as you move through the lessons presented in this book).

In my experience, writing a voice-over script is easier than writing a step-by-step script for recording a software simulation (voice-over scripts typically take me 50 percent less time to write). If you spent 80 hours writing the script, you should budget 40 hours to write the voice-over script.

Once the voice-over script is done, you'll also need to include time for recording the audio narration (voice-overs), making corrections to the step-by-step script post-rehearsal, and recording the lessons using Captivate (the recording time should take the same amount of time as the process being recorded).

It could easily take 10 hours to produce a five-minute Captivate lesson. During the production process, you will likely need to add and/or edit text captions (which you will learn about beginning on page 85). Typical Captivate projects include interactive objects, such as Click Boxes (page 181), Buttons (page 34), and Text Entry Boxes (page 185). And a typical project should include a quiz to measure learner comprehension of the content (you will learn about quizzes beginning on page 199).

During the production process, you'll likely add audio clips to the project's background, individual slides, and even objects on individual slides. It's also likely that you'll either record voice-over audio (or use Captivate's Text to Speech feature to convert written text to voice-over audio. And you'll likely need to edit the audio files by performing such common tasks as removing unwanted noise. (You will learn to work with audio on page 141.)

Finally, you'll need to publish the finished project into any one of several output formats, possibly uploading those files to a server or Learning Management System (LMS) and testing for scoring or interactivity errors. After that, you'll need to fix problems (and there will likely be plenty of problems that need to be fixed). After fixing those problems, you'll need to republish, repost, and then retest. (You will learn to Publish projects beginning on page 233.)

Your eLearning development budget (to create a 60-minute eLearning course) might look something like this:

- ❑ 40-80 hours to write an eLearning script or create the storyboard to support 12, five-minute lessons for a one-hour course.

- ❑ 120 hours to edit, produce, and test 12, five-minute lessons (two-hours for every minute of playtime).

- ❑ 20-40 hours to write a narration script to be used by your narrator.

- ❑ 20-40 hours to record and enhance voice narration (less if you use Text to Speech, which you will learn about on page 162).

NOTES

Project Size and Display Resolution

When you create a blank Captivate project or record a software simulation, you'll need to set the project's width and height. Several years ago, monitors were small and display resolutions were low. In fact, a display resolution of 800 x 600 pixels was common. If you developed eLearning content for a display that small, a project size of 640 x 480 was ideal. A few years later, 1024 x 768 was the standard display resolution, resulting in typical eLearning lessons sized to 800 x 600.

According to **w3schools.com** (https://www.w3schools.com/browsers/browsers_display.asp), the standard desktop screen resolution today is **1366 x 768 or higher**. (You'll find that available resolutions vary from system to system. For instance, I use an HP 22-inch display that doesn't support 1366 x 768. Instead, my closest options are 1360 x 768 and 1376 x 812.)

Because screen resolutions are higher than ever, many eLearning developers are seeking an optimal viewing experience for learners. But what's the ideal size for an eLearning lesson? Unfortunately, there isn't a cookie-cutter answer. The size of the lesson you create depends largely on the size of your display and its resolution. If you are recording a software simulation, the size of your project might be dependent upon the size of the software you're recording (some software cannot be resized and may to take up your whole display).

There's more to consider when it comes to project size. What kind of device are your learners using? How big is their display? Is their device typically used vertically (portrait) or horizontally (landscape)? What is the typical size of an iPad? How about a Surface Pro?

If you are creating content for learners using standard desktop computers (Windows or Mac), your 800 x 600 project might look fine. However, if you upload your content to YouTube, 800 x 600 won't look right (you will see black bars on one or both sides of the video, and the video might look distorted during playback).

Selecting an ideal project size is a delicate balancing act between the size of the capture area and an ideal screen resolution. When I create YouTube videos, I set Captivate's recording size to 1280 x 720 and my computer's screen resolution fairly high. Although I could go higher with my screen resolution and capture more of my screen, the captured screen text at a higher screen resolution tends to be small and difficult for most people to read.

When the time comes to Publish your Captivate project, there is an option called **Scalable HTML content**.

☑ Scalable HTML content

When you publish your project with Scalable HTML content enabled, learners with large screens similar to yours will see your lesson pretty much at full size. For other learners, the lesson will automatically scale up or down to fit their screen. In short, Scalable HTML content takes away much of the anxiety you'll have to contend with when it comes to project size. For that reason, I encourage you to consider using Scalable HTML Content when publishing.

Also, when developing your eLearning courses, consider using a font and font size that remains readable when resized for a small screen. Imagine how tiny the text could become if a learner uses a device with a small screen such as a smart phone.

Designing Slides in Captivate

As you begin to work in Captivate to develop standard (not video) projects, the program will likely seem very familiar to you... sort of like Microsoft PowerPoint. If you've used PowerPoint you are familiar with the Filmstrip showing miniatures of the slides along the left side of the PowerPoint interface. Captivate is similar. In fact, like PowerPoint, you create individual slides in Captivate and populate those slides with text, images, animation... just about anything.

You don't have to be a seasoned designer to produce beautiful and effective Captivate slides. Here are a few tips to get you started:

- ❒ There are occasions when a bulleted list is the best way to convey an idea. Although PowerPoint uses a bulleted approach to information by default, you do not have to use that format in eLearning.

- ❒ Try splitting the bullets into separate slides with a single image to illustrate each point, or forgo the text altogether and replace it with a chart, diagram, or other informative image.

- ❒ It is not necessary to have every bit of information you cover on one slide. Encourage your audience to listen and, if necessary, take notes based on what you say, not what is shown on the slide.

- ❒ Nothing says "High School Presentation Circa 1997" quite like a dancing animated image clumsily plopped on a rainbow gradient background with a big, garish image.

- ❒ Few learners are impressed with how many moving, colorful objects each slide contains. When it comes to eLearning, the old saying, "content is King," has never been more appropriate. Ensure each of your slides contains relevant, need-to-know information and that the information is presented as clutter-free as possible.

- ❒ Consider taking more of a photographic approach to the images you use. You can easily find stock photographs on the web using any one of a number of pay-for-use websites. There are many free sites, but keep in mind that to save time and frustration (and improve on the selection and quality), you might want to set aside a budget to pay for images.

Fonts and eLearning

There is no denying that the most important thing about eLearning is solid content. But could you be inadvertently making your content harder to read and understand by using the wrong fonts? Is good font selection really important? Read on to discover the many surprising ways fonts can affect your content.

Some Fonts Read Better On-Screen

eCommerce Consultant Dr. Ralph F. Wilson did a study in 2001 to determine if serif fonts (fonts with little lines on the tops and bottoms of characters, such as Times New Roman) or sans serif fonts (those without lines, such as Arial) were more suited to being read on computer monitors. His study concluded that although Times New Roman is easily read in printed materials, the lower resolution of monitors (72 dots per inch (dpi) versus 180 dpi or higher) makes it much more difficult to read in digital format. Arial 12 pt was pitted against Times New Roman 12 pt with respondents finding the sans serif Arial font more readable at a rate of two to one.

Lorem ipsum frangali puttuto rigali fortuitous confulence magficati alorem. Lorem ipsum frangali puttuto rigali fortuitous confulence magficati alorem.	Lorem ipsum frangali puttuto rigali fortuitous confulence magficati alorem. Lorem ipsum frangali puttuto rigali fortuitous confulence magficati alorem.
Times New Roman 12 pt	Arial 12 pt
520	1123
32%	68%

Source: http://www.practicalecommerce.com/html-email-fonts

Wilson also tested the readability of Arial versus Verdana on computer screens and found that in font sizes greater than 10 pt, Arial was more readable, whereas Verdana was more readable in font sizes 10 pt and smaller.

So should you stop using Times New Roman in your eLearning lessons? Not completely. For instance, you can still use Times New Roman for text content that is not expected to be skimmed over quickly or read in a hurry.

Some Fonts Increase Trust

A 2008 study by Sharath Sasidharan and Ganga Dhanesh for the Association of Information Systems found that typography can affect trust in eCommerce. The study found that to instill trust in online consumers, you should keep it simple: "To the extent possible, particularly for websites that need to engage in financial transactions or collect personal information from their users, the dominant typeface used to present text material should be a serif or sans serif font such as Times New Roman or Arial."

If you feel your eLearning content will be presented to a skeptical audience (or one you've never worked with before), dazzling them with fancy fonts may not be the way to go. You can use fancy fonts from time to time to break up the monotony of a dry lesson, but consider using such non-standard fonts sparingly. Use the fancy fonts for headings or as accents but not for the bulk of your text.

The Readability of Fonts Affects Participation

A study done at the University of Michigan in 2008 on typecase in instructions found that the ease with which a font in instructional material is read can have an impact on the perceived skill level needed to complete a task.

The study found that if directions are presented in a font that is deemed more difficult to read, "the task will be viewed as being difficult, taking a long time to complete and perhaps, not even worth trying."

The results of the study by Wilson indicate that it is probably not a good idea to present eLearning material, especially to beginners, in a Times New Roman font, as it may make the information seem too difficult to process or overwhelming.

Popular eLearning Fonts

I polled my "Skills & Drills" newsletter readers and asked which fonts they tended to use in eLearning. Here is a list of the most popular fonts:

- ☐ Verdana
- ☐ Helvetica
- ☐ Arial
- ☐ Calibri
- ☐ Times
- ☐ Palatino
- ☐ Times New Roman
- ☐ Century Schoolbook (for print)

Fonts and Personas

If you are creating eLearning for business professionals, you might want to use a different font in your design than you would if you were creating eLearning for high school students. But what font would you use if you want to convey a feeling of happiness? Formality? Cuddliness?

In a study (funded by Microsoft) by A. Dawn Shaikh, Barbara S. Chaparro, and Doug Fox, the perceived personality traits of fonts were categorized. The table below shows the top three fonts for each personality objective.

	Top Three		
Stable	TNR	Arial	Cambria
Flexible	Kristen	Gigi	Rage Italic
Conformist	Courier New	TNR	Arial
Polite	Monotype Corsiva	TNR	Cambria
Mature	TNR	Courier New	Cambria
Formal	TNR	Monotype Corsiva	Georgia
Assertive	**Impact**	**Rockwell Xbold**	Georgia
Practical	Georgia	TNR	Cambria
Creative	Gigi	Kristen	Rage Italic
Happy	Kristen	Gigi	Comic Sans
Exciting	Gigi	Kristen	Rage Italic
Attractive	Monotype Corsiva	Rage Italic	Gigi
Elegant	Monotype Corsiva	Rage Italic	Gigi
Cuddly	Kristen	Gigi	Comic Sans
Feminine	Gigi	Monotype Corsiva	Kristen
Unstable	Gigi	Kristen	Rage Italic
Rigid	**Impact**	Courier New	Agency FB
Rebel	Gigi	Kristen	Rage Italic
Rude	**Impact**	**Rockwell Xbold**	Agency FB
Youthful	Kristen	Gigi	Comic Sans
Casual	Kristen	Comic Sans	Gigi
Passive	Kristen	Gigi	Comic Sans
Impractical	Gigi	Rage Italic	Kristen
Unimaginative	Courier New	Arial	Consolas
Sad	**Impact**	Courier New	Agency FB
Dull	Courier New	Consolas	Verdana
Unattractive	**Impact**	Courier New	**Rockwell Xbold**
Plain	Courier New	**Impact**	**Rockwell Xbold**
Coarse	**Impact**	**Rockwell Xbold**	Courier New
Masculine	**Impact**	**Rockwell Xbold**	Courier New

Source: http://apo.org.au/system/files/17225/apo-nid17225-100061.pdf

Module 1: Exploring Captivate

In This Module You Will Learn About:

- The Captivate Interface, page 14
- Previewing, page 21

And You Will Learn To:

- Explore a Finished Captivate Project, page 14
- Zoom and Magnify, page 16
- Navigate a Project, page 17
- Explore and Reset the Workspace, page 19
- Preview the Entire Project, page 21

The Captivate Interface

As you work through the lessons in this book, the goal is to get you comfortable with specific Captivate areas or features before proceeding. Like any feature-rich program, mastering Captivate is going to be a marathon, not a sprint. Soon enough you'll be in full stride, creating awesome eLearning content using Captivate. But before the sprint comes the crawl.

During these first few activities, I'd like to give you a chance to familiarize yourself with Captivate's user interface. Specifically, you'll be instructed to start Captivate, open an existing project, and poke around Captivate's interface a bit.

Guided Activity 1: Explore a Finished Captivate Project

1. Start Adobe Captivate.

   The process of starting a program varies slightly from operating system to operating system. Because Captivate is available for both the Macintosh and Windows, I'll leave it to you to start the program using any technique you're comfortable with.

   If this is your first time starting Captivate, the first thing you'll likely see is an Introduction Video highlighting some of Captivate's cool features. You can either watch the video in its entirety or dismiss the video by clicking the Close button.

   Next, you'll see the **Home** screen consisting of three tabs: **Recent, New**, and **Resources**. The Recent tab will be blank until after you have opened or created a project. Shown below is the Home screen for the Windows version of Adobe Captivate.

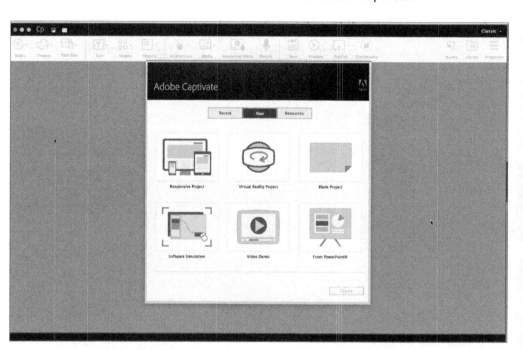

   Captivate 2019 is nearly identical on the Windows and Macintosh operating systems. Nevertheless, there are some differences between the two versions and I'll point them out as appropriate.

   Note: You are about to be asked to open a Captivate project from the **Captivate2019** data folder—assets that support the lessons in this book. If you have not yet downloaded and installed the Captivate2019Data folder, turn to the

About This Book Section at the beginning of this book and complete the "Data Files (Captivate Project Assets)" activity that begins on page ix before moving on to the next step.

2. Open a project from the **Captivate2019Data** folder.

   ☐ on the **Home** screen, click the **Recent** tab

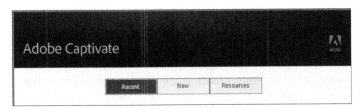

   ☐ from the bottom left of the tab, click the **Browse** button

   The **Open** dialog box appears.

   ☐ navigate to the **Captivate2019Data** folder and open **AceInterview.cptx**

   Note: Most of the projects you will open as you work through this book were created in older versions of Captivate and upgraded to the current version. All of the projects use web safe, standard fonts. Should you receive a message about missing fonts, no worries. Click the **Replace Fonts** button and move on.

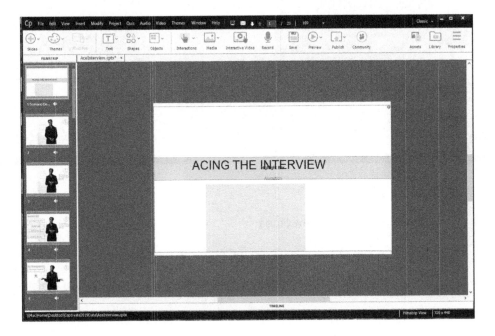

3. Close the project and reopen it using the Recent tab.

   ☐ choose **File > Close** (do not save the project if prompted)

   ☐ on the Captivate **Home** screen, click the **Recent** tab

   Once you've opened and then closed a project, the **Recent** tab gives you quick access to those recently used projects.

   ☐ double-click **AceInterview** to reopen the project

Guided Activity 2: Zoom and Magnify

1. Ensure that the **AceInterview** project is still open.

2. Zoom away from a slide.

   ☐ choose **View > Magnification > 50%**

   You can zoom as far away as 25 percent and as up close and personal as 600 percent. At a 50 percent view, it's a good bet you can see the Filmstrip at the left, a slide in the middle of the Captivate window, and a gray area surrounding the slide. The gray area is known as the **Pasteboard**. You can drop any slide object on the Pasteboard and leave it there indefinitely. When an object is on the Pasteboard, it will not appear in the published version of your lesson, nor will it preview (you'll learn to both publish and preview later).

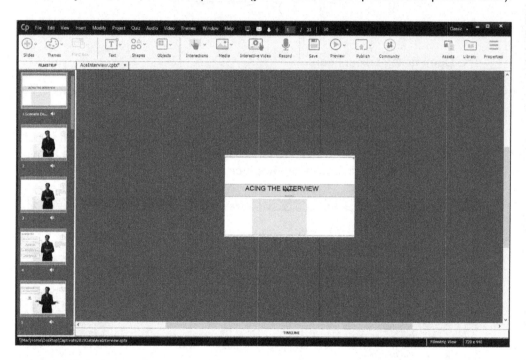

3. Zoom closer to a slide.

   ☐ choose **View > Zoom in** a few times

   As you select the Zoom in command, you get closer to the slide.

   ☐ choose **View > Zoom in** two or three more times to get a little closer to the slide

4. Change the slide zoom to Best Fit.

   ☐ choose **View > Magnification > Best Fit**

Guided Activity 3: Navigate a Project

1. Ensure that the AceInterview project is still open.

2. Set your **View** magnification to a view that works best for you and your display.

3. Switch slides using the Filmstrip.

   ☐ at the left of the Captivate window, scroll the **Filmstrip** as necessary until you see the thumbnail view of slide **7**

   ☐ on the **Filmstrip**, click one time on slide **7** to view the slide in the middle of the Captivate window

Once a slide is open in the main area of the Captivate window, you can select any of the slide's objects and manipulate them. For instance, you can edit slide text, add images, delete images, add a button, change an object's timing, etc. If you need to change the attributes of one or more slides, you do not need to have it open within the main Captivate interface. Instead, you can select multiple slides on the Filmstrip and change their Properties at one time.

4. Jump to a slide using the Go to slide field.

   ☐ from the Captivate menu bar at the top of the window, highlight the number you see in the current slide Page Number field

   ☐ type any slide number between **1** and **23**

Note: If you don't see the Page Number field as shown in the image above, try enlarging the Captivate window. When the Captivate window is small, some menu items are cropped from view.

5. Jump between slides using your keyboard.

    ☐ with any of the slides on the Filmstrip selected, press either [**page up**] or [**page down**] on your keyboard

    As you press the keys, notice that you quickly move from slide to slide.

    Note: If you are using a Macintosh laptop, such as a MacBook Pro without [**page up**] or [**page down**] keys, try pressing the **up** and **down** arrows on the lower right of your keyboard to move from slide to slide. On some newer computers, the Up arrow was replaced with **Page Up**; the Down arrow was replaced with **Page Down**; the Left arrow with **Home**; and the Right arrow with **End**.

Guided Activity 4: Explore and Reset the Workspace

1. Ensure that the AceInterview project is still open.

2. Explore the Properties Inspector and the Library.

   ☐ from the top right of the Captivate window, click **Properties**

   A panel opens at the right of the Captivate window. As you move through the lessons in this book, you'll be using this area frequently. I've heard people refer to the panels in Captivate by all kinds of names. Is it a pod? Is it a panel? Is it Superman? (I just dated myself with that one.) I promise that there won't be a test about this stuff later, so pick a name for these Captivate areas that works for you. According to my contact at Adobe, an individual panel is known as an Inspector, so clicking Properties actually displays two inspectors: **Properties** and **Timing**.

   ☐ from the top right of the Captivate window, click **Library**

   The Library, which keeps tabs of many of a project's assets (such as images and audio), takes the place of the Properties Inspector. You'll learn to use the Library beginning on page 124.

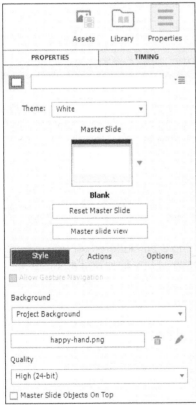

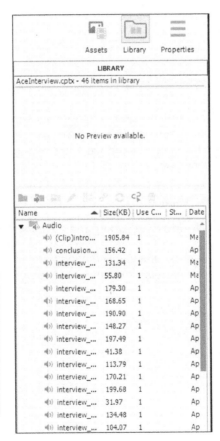

Above, the Properties Inspector. At the right, the Library.

NOTES

---

3. Explore the Timeline.

❏ from the bottom center of the Captivate window, click **Timeline**

The Timeline appears at the bottom of the Captivate window. You'll learn how to work with the Timeline beginning on page 96.

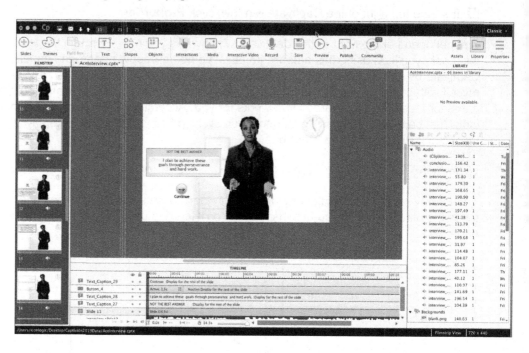

With the Timeline and Library open, your screen is a bit more... complicated. Although all of these open inspectors/panels are useful, it's a good idea to know how to get yourself back to the nice, clean interface you saw a few moments ago. Next you'll learn how to reset the workspace.

4. Reset the workspace.

❏ choose **Window > Workspace > Reset 'Classic'**

If you ever feel like the Captivate interface is getting a bit cluttered, or you cannot find standard pods/panels, you can reset the workspace at any time and as often as you like.

Previewing

You will learn how to develop several eLearning lessons using Captivate. You will finish the development process by publishing (you will learn how to Publish beginning on page 233). Once published, the eLearning lesson can be used (consumed) by people using all kinds of devices (including desktop computers and mobile devices, such as the iPad or the Kindle Fire). Prior to publishing, it's a good idea to preview the project so you can see how the lesson looks once published. There are multiple preview options, including Play Slide, Project, From this Slide, Next 5 slides, In Browser, and HTML5 in Browser. Because previewing the Project shows a quick version of a published project without starting a web browser and Next 5 slides quickly shows just a few slides at a time, I find those two options to be the most useful.

Guided Activity 5: Preview the Entire Project

1. Ensure that the **AceInterview** project is still open.

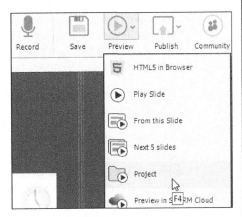

2. Preview the project.

   ❑ from the **Toolbar** at the top of the Captivate window, click **Preview**

   ❑ choose **Project** from the menu

   The lesson is generated and then begins to play.

   After several seconds, the fourth slide stops and waits for you to interact with it.

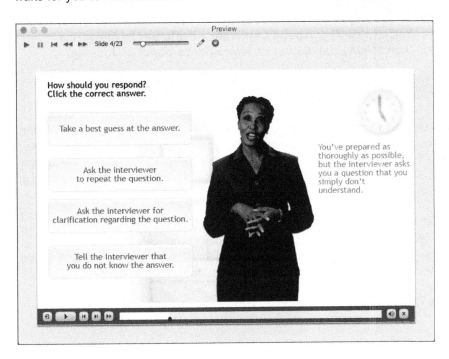

NOTES

Previewing Confidence Check

1. Continue working through the preview.

2. When you are finished interacting with the lesson (you do not need to watch it in its entirety), click the **End** button on the toolbar at the top of the preview.

3. Preview the project as **SWF in Browser**.

   A Flash preview of the lesson (as it will appear via the learner's web browser) opens in your default web browser. If SWF in Browser does not work it likely means that your browser is being blocked from viewing SWF (Flash) content. In that case, preview as **HTML5 in Browser** instead, click **Yes** when warned about supported objects.

4. Close the browser window when you are done exploring. (There is no need to go through the entire lesson.)

   Note: You might have noticed that you cannot drag the Inspectors around your screen like you can in other programs. Because there are so many Inspectors in Captivate, it's generally a good idea to leave the Captivate interface alone. However, if you have multiple monitors, you might want to put a few Inspectors on one monitor and your main Captivate window on another monitor. If you'd like to move your Inspectors around the screen, you can create custom workspaces. Open Captivate's Preferences dialog box by choosing **Edit > Preferences** (if you're a Windows user) or **Adobe Captivate > Preferences** (if you're a Mac user). Then select **Enable custom workspaces/panel undocking**.

   ☐ Enable custom workspaces/panel undocking (you will need to restart Captivate)

   Click the **OK** button to close the dialog box and then restart Captivate. You'll then be able to move several of the panels around your screen (even across multiple screens). If you like your new workspace, you can keep it by choosing **Window > Workspace > Save Workspace**. Once saved, your new workspace is available in the Workspace sub-menu.

   While custom workspaces are great, they can clutter the Captivate environment. To avoid the clutter, I'll avoid custom workspaces completely in this book. I encourage you to work through this book using the Classic workspace and create custom workspaces only once you feel more comfortable with Adobe Captivate.

5. Close the Captivate project (there is no need to save if prompted).

iCONLOGiC
"Skills and Drills" Learning

Module 2: New Projects

In This Module You Will Learn About:

- Soft Skills eLearning, page 24
- Buttons, page 34

And You Will Learn To:

- Create a Blank Project, page 24
- Add Images to Placeholders, page 29
- Import Images, page 32
- Use a Smart Shape as a Button, page 34
- Disable Click Sounds, page 37

Soft Skills eLearning

You can use Adobe Captivate to record actions you perform on your computer. Those recordings can be interactive (often referred to as "Let Me Try" eLearning), demos (often referred to as "Show Me" eLearning), and videos (much like the kind you've likely seen on YouTube or Vimeo).

Soft Skills eLearning encompasses anything that doesn't fall into the category of a computer recording. Over the years, I've helped my clients develop soft skills lessons covering all kinds of topics, including onboarding, terrorism awareness, compliance training, conflict resolution, and policies and procedures. Anything that's a life skill would fall into the category of soft skills.

During the lessons in this module, you will create a soft skills lesson that introduces employees of an imaginary company called Biff's Bakery. The managers you will add to the lesson don't exist either. Made-up content or not, the project you are about to create will include multiple slides, text captions, and images. You will also add interactive buttons to the slides using Smart Shapes allowing learners to move through the lesson at their own pace.

Guided Activity 6: Create a Blank Project

1. Create a blank project.

    ☐ using Adobe Captivate, choose **File > New Project > Blank Project**

    The New Blank Project dialog box opens.

2. Specify a Width and Height for the project.

    ☐ from the **Select** drop-down menu, choose **1280 x 720**

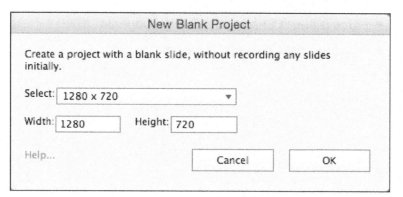

    ☐ click the **OK** button

    Your new project contains a single slide. Visually-speaking the slide isn't much to look at. That will change shortly after you apply a theme to the project. (A theme is a collection of master slides, placeholders, objects, and styles that help keep your slides looking consistent throughout an entire project.)

3. Save the new project.

    ☐ choose **File > Save**

    ☐ name the project **OurManagers**

    ☐ save the file to the **Captivate2019Data** folder

4. Add content to slide placeholders.

   ☐ if necessary, zoom **out** so that you can see most of the slide

   ☐ on the slide, double-click the title placeholder where it says "Double click to add title"

   ☐ replace the placeholder text with **Biff's Bakery: The Management Team**

Biff's Bakery: The Management Team

5. Apply a theme.

   ☐ from the **left** side of the **Toolbar**, click the **Themes** tool

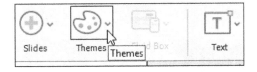

   ☐ roll your cursor over the themes to display their names

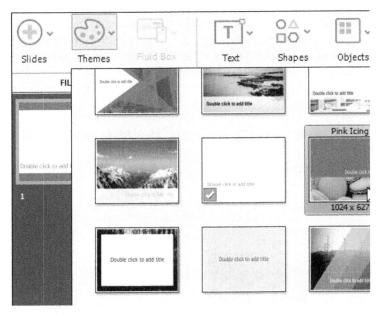

❑ select the Theme called **Pink Icing**

You will be prompted to confirm the action.

❑ click the **Yes** button

The existing slide takes on the appearance of the Pink Icing theme. And by applying a theme, each new slide you add during the next steps will be formatted using the attributes of that theme.

Note: If you don't see the Pink Icing theme, click the **Browse** link in the lower left of the Themes and find the themes collection on your computer. Windows users, browse to **eLearning Assets\Layouts\11_5\en_US**. Mac users, browse to **Documents\My Adobe Captivate Projects\Layouts\ 11_5\en_US**.

6. Insert a new slide.

❑ from the toolbar at the top of the Captivate window, click **Slides** and choose **Content Slide**

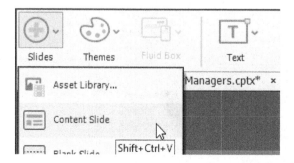

7. Apply a different Master Slide to the new slide to change its appearance.

   ☐ ensure the second slide is selected on the **Filmstrip**

   ☐ at the right side of the Captivate window, click **Properties** to display the **Properties Inspector**

   ☐ on the **Properties Inspector**, **Master Slide** area, click the Master Slide **thumbnail** and from the drop-down menu choose **Content 07**

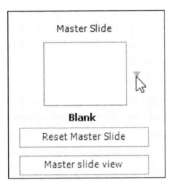 

The new slide takes on the appearance of the **Content 7** master slide and contains some placeholders for slide content.

8. Apply a different Master Slide to the new slide.

   ☐ on the **Filmstrip**, ensure the second slide is selected

   ☐ on the **Properties Inspector**, **Master Slide** area, click the drop-down menu and choose **Content 01**

New Slides Confidence Check

1. Still working on slide **2** of the OurManagers project, replace the subtitle placeholder with **Lesson Overview**.

2. Replace the caption placeholder with **During this lesson, you will learn about our key managers.**

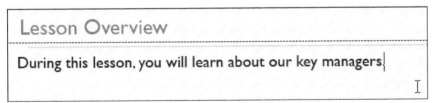

Note: It's not necessary to delete unused placeholders. If you don't add anything within a placeholder, the placeholder object will not be included when you preview or publish the project.

3. Insert a **New Content Slide** that uses the **Content 01** layout.

4. Replace the subtitle placeholder text with **Lesson Review**.

5. Replace the next placeholder with **During this lesson, you learned about our key managers. In particular, you learned that while Biff takes credit for making the company the most successful of its kind in the world, it's really Betty who deserves all of the credit.**

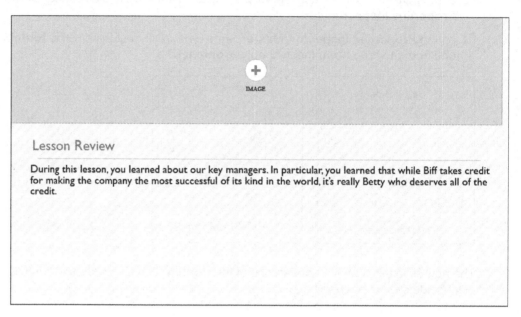

6. Save your work and keep the project open for the next activity.

Guided Activity 7: Add Images to Placeholders

1. Ensure that the **OurManagers** project is still open.

2. Insert an image into an image placeholder.

   ☐ on the **Filmstrip**, select slide **2**

   ☐ at the top of the slide, double-click the **plus sign** (the image placeholder)

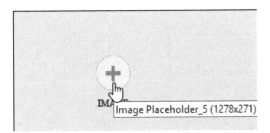

The **Select Image from Library** dialog box opens.

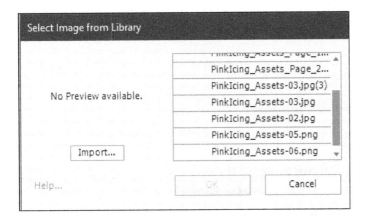

   ☐ at the left of the dialog box, click the **Import** button

   ☐ from the **Captivate2019Data** folder, open the **images** folder

   ☐ open the **bakery-banner** image

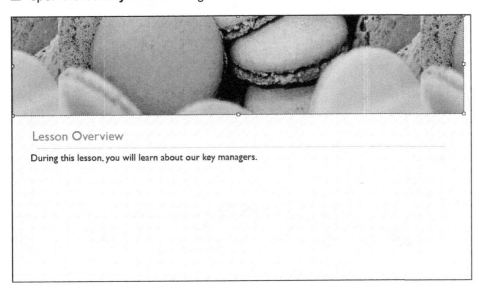

NOTES

Text and Image Placeholders
Confidence Check

1. On slide 3, insert the **bakery-banner** image into the image placeholder.

   Note: Because you have already inserted the bakery-banner image into the project, you'll find the image is already listed among the Library assets and you can use it instead of reimporting.

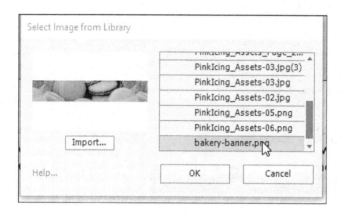

2. Select slide 2 on the Filmstrip.

3. Insert a new slide that uses the **Content 07** layout.

4. Ensure you are working on the new slide and replace the subtitle text with **Biff Bifferson: President**

5. Replace the caption text with **Biff founded the company in 1993 with just $55 in the bank. Today, the company is worth in excess of $10 billion**.

6. Add a few line breaks in the text you just typed by clicking in front of the word "Today" and pressing [**enter**] twice.

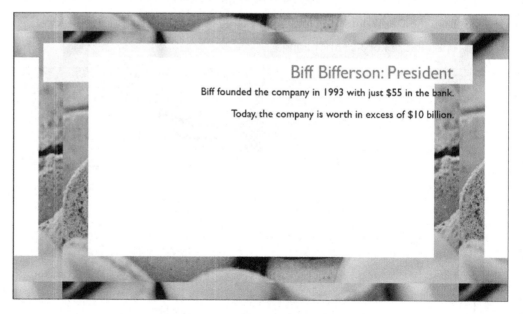

7. Select slide **3** and insert a new slide based on **Content 07**.

8. Replace the subtitle placeholder with **Betty Bifferson: Vice President**.

9. Replace the next placeholder with **Betty joined the company in 1995. She is really the brains behind the operation.**

10. Add line breaks to make your slide match the image below.

Guided Activity 8: Import Images

1. Ensure that the **OurManagers** project is still open.

2. Import an image without a placeholder.

   ☐ on the **Filmstrip**, select slide **3** (the Biff Bifferson slide)

   ☐ from the toolbar at the top of the Captivate window, click **Media** and choose **Image**

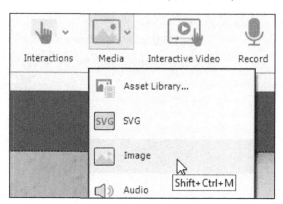

   ☐ from the **Captivate2019Data** folder, open **images**

   ☐ open the **biff_baby** image

   ☐ position the image similar to what is shown below

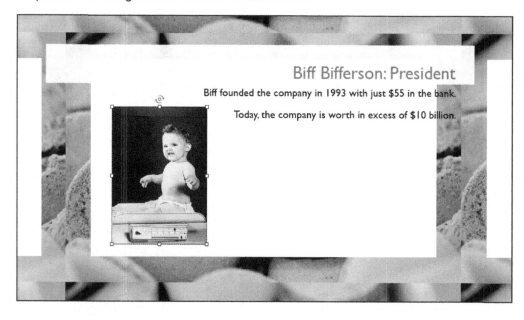

Import Media Confidence Check

1. On slide 4, import the betty_baby image and position it similar to what is shown below.

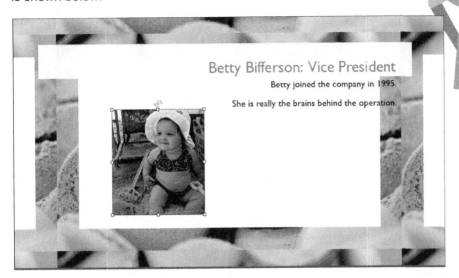

2. Preview the project **in Browser** as either **HTML5** or **SWF**. (You learned how to Preview on page 21.)

   The lesson automatically moves from slide to slide. When the lesson is finished, you can use the playbar at the bottom of the window to rewind.

   If this is your first eLearning project, congratulations are in order. Although the project is simple, it is an eLearning lesson nevertheless. Take a bow, you're on your way to eLearning greatness!

3. When finished previewing, close the browser window.

4. Spend a few moments applying a few of the other Themes to your project and take note of how the Theme designs impact your current slide layouts.

1. When finished, save and close the project.

NOTES

Buttons

Buttons serve two crucial roles. First, buttons stop slides from moving forward on their own. Using **Actions**, you control what happens when the learner successfully clicks a button (such as **Go to the next slide** or **Play Audio**). There are multiple types of buttons: Text, Transparent, Image, and Shape. During the following activities, you'll insert a shape and use it as a button.

Guided Activity 9: Use a Smart Shape as a Button

1. Using Captivate, open **ButtonMe** from the **Captivate2019Data** folder.

2. Insert a Smart Shape onto the slide.

   ❑ ensure that you are on slide **1**

   ❑ from the toolbar, click **Shapes** and, from the **Arrows** group, choose **Right Arrow**

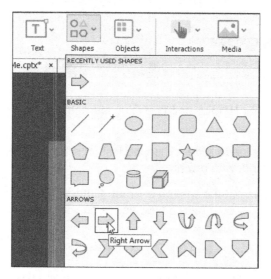

   ❑ on the slide, draw a right arrow similar to the one shown in the image below

If you're a PowerPoint user, you've long appreciated the ability to draw just about any kind of shape you need on your slides using AutoShapes. In Captivate, you have a similar

ability via the Smart Shapes feature. You'll find myriad shapes from which to choose, including Callouts, Banners, and other wacky shapes.

☐ double-click the arrow on the slide and type **Begin**

☐ click away from the arrow (to exit text edit mode) and then drag the arrow until its position is similar to the picture below.

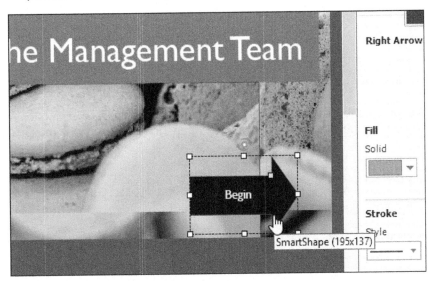

3. Change the arrow into an interactive button.

☐ on the slide, select the arrow

☐ on the **Properties Inspector**, look just below the **Style Name** area

☐ select **Use as Button**

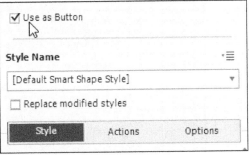

4. Review the button's Action.

☐ with the arrow shape selected, select the **Actions** tab on the **Properties Inspector**

An Action occurs after the learner has clicked an interactive object. In this instance, when the learner successfully clicks the shape, you want the learner to go to the next slide. Therefore, the **On Success** action of **Go to the next slide** is perfect. This is the default action for most interactive objects.

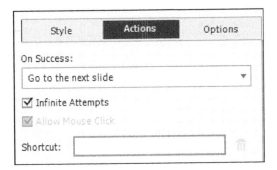

NOTES

5. Add a Hand Cursor to the button.

☐ ensure that the arrow/button is still selected

☐ on the **Actions** tab, **Others** area, select **Hand Cursor**

Others

☐ Pause for Success/Failure Captions
☑ Hand Cursor
☐ Double-click
☐ Disable Click Sound

A Hand Cursor lets the learner know that the button is clickable by changing the appearance of the mouse cursor to a hand icon when the learner runs the mouse over the button.

6. Preview the Project.

☐ on the Toolbar, click **Preview** and choose **Project**

As the first slide plays, notice that the button prevents the slide from moving forward on its own.

☐ click the button to move to the second slide

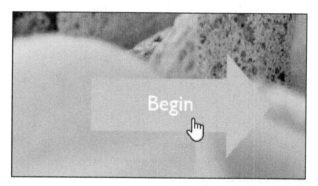

Assuming you have speakers or are wearing a headset, did you notice that there was a click sound that accompanied the button? Some people like the click sound, others do not. Assuming you do not like the click sound, you will learn how to remove it next.

7. Close the preview.

Guided Activity 10: Disable Click Sounds

1. Ensure that the **ButtonMe** project is still open.

2. Disable a button's Click Sound.

   ☐ on slide 1, select the **arrow/button**

   ☐ on the Properties Inspector, **Actions** tab, **Others** area, select **Disable Click Sound**

3. Preview the Project.

4. Click the button to move to the second slide.

   Upon clicking the button, notice that the click sound has been removed.

5. Close the preview.

Buttons Confidence Check

1. Still working in the ButtonMe project, copy the button you added to slide 1 to the clipboard.

2. On the Filmstrip, select slide **2**.

3. Paste the button onto the selected slide.

4. Double-click the button and change the text to **Next**.

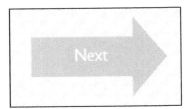

5. Deselect the button (to exit text-edit mode) and then copy the edited button to the clipboard.

6. Select slides 3, 4, and 5 (selecting one slide and [shift]-clicking works great for selected multiple slides)

7. Paste the button onto the selected slides.

   The cool thing about copying and pasting slide objects is that, in addition to getting the object on several slides at once, the pasted objects are all in the same slide location.

8. Go to slide **5** change the text on the button to **Replay**.

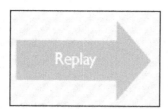

9. Click away from the button to exit text edit mode.

10. Go back and right-click the button and choose **Replace Smart Shape**.

11. From the Arrows group, choose **Left Arrow**.

12. Using the Actions tab on the Properties Inspector, change the **On Success** Action for the button to **Jump to slide**.

13. Select **1 Slide 1** as the destination.

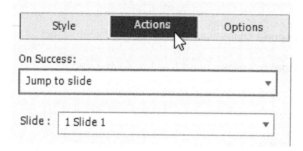

14. Preview the project.

    There should be interactive buttons on each slide allowing you to control how fast or slow you move through the lesson.

15. When you get to the last slide, click the **Replay** button to go back to the beginning of the lesson.

16. Close the preview.

17. Save and close the project.

Module 3: Screen Recordings

In This Module You Will Learn About:

And You Will Learn To:

Preparing to Record a Software Simulation

Standard Captivate projects consist of individual slides, similar to Microsoft PowerPoint. You can create a blank Captivate project and insert slides, just like you learned to do beginning on page 24. If you need to capture a software application, you can use any one of several programs. For instance, I used SnagIt for the Macintosh (**www.snagit.com**) and FullShot (**www.fullshot.com**) for Windows to create the Captivate screen captures in this book. Individual screen captures can be inserted onto any Captivate slide as an image.

As an alternative to using a third-party application to create screen captures, you can use Captivate to record just about anything you do on your computer. Captivate offers three recording types: Automatic, Manual, and Video. If you use Captivate's Automatic recording type, Captivate captures the steps you take on your computer by creating a screen capture every time you click your mouse. There are four Automatic capture modes: Demonstration, Assessment Simulation, Training Simulation, and Custom. Each mode is covered during this module.

If you create projects using the Manual recording type, you are responsible for pressing a specific key on your keyboard each time you want Captivate to create a screen capture (the default key is the Print Screen key in Windows). The problem with recording projects using the Manual Recording method is that you need to be very diligent about pressing the screen capture key on your keyboard. You could easily get distracted and forget to capture important screens, rendering your recording useless and requiring you to recapture some or all of your clicks.

Using the Video recording type, Captivate does not capture individual screens like the Automatic and Manual types. Instead, when the capture process is finished, you end up with a single video demonstrating everything you have done during the recording process. A video recording is ideal if you are trying to create an eLearning lesson demonstrating complex mouse actions (like those that would be required when drawing a shape in an image-editing application). However, editing a video is more limited as compared to editing individual screen captures typical in projects created using the Automatic or Manual recording types.

In the images below, both the Automatic and Manual recording types are shown at the left. Video mode is shown at the right. (**Note:** The Automatic, Manual, and Video modes are all covered in this book.)

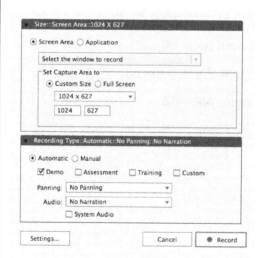

Rehearsals

You have been hired to create an eLearning course that teaches new employees at your company how to use **Notepad** (Windows) or **TextEdit** (Macintosh). One of the lessons you plan to record using Captivate includes how to change the page orientation within Notepad or TextEdit.

Here is a sample script showing the kind of detailed, step-by-step instructions you need to create or receive from a Subject Matter Expert (SME). You are expected to perform each step written below in either Notepad or TextEdit.

Dear Captivate developer, using either Notepad or TextEdit, record the process of changing the Page Orientation from Portrait to Landscape, and then back again (from Landscape to Portrait). Create the recording using a capture size of 800 x 600. Thanks. Your pal, the Subject Matter Expert.

1. Click the File menu.

2. Click the Page Setup menu item.

3. Click the Landscape orientation button.

4. Click the OK button.

5. Click the File menu.

6. Click the Page Setup menu item.

7. Click the Portrait orientation button.

8. Click the OK button.

9. Stop the recording process.

The script sounds simple. However, you will not know what kind of trouble you are going to get into unless you rehearse the script prior to recording the process with Captivate. Let's run a rehearsal, just as if you were a big-time movie director and you were in charge of a blockbuster movie.

Places everyone... and quiet on the set...

Guided Activity 11: Rehearse a Script

1. Minimize (hide) Captivate.

2. Start either Notepad (Windows) or TextEdit (Mac).

   The process of starting either Notepad or TextEdit varies slightly depending on your operating system. For instance, if you are using Windows 7, choose **Start**, type **notepad**, and press [**enter**]. If you are using Windows 8 or newer, use the **Search** feature to find and open Notepad. If you are using a Mac, choose **Go > Applications**. Locate and then open **TextEdit**, and then create a **New** document.

   In the images below, Notepad is pictured at the left; TextEdit is at the right.

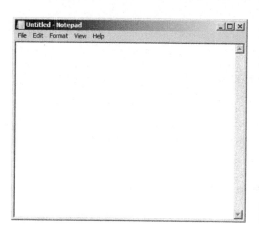
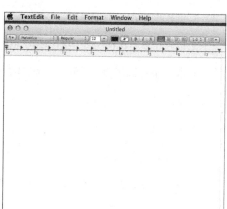

3. Rehearse the script.

   ❑ using either Notepad or TextEdit (not Captivate), click the **File** menu

   ❑ click the **Page Setup** menu item

   ❑ from the **Orientation** area, click **Landscape**

   Note: In Notepad, Landscape is listed as the word "Landscape." In TextEdit, Landscape is the **second** tool (shown below).

   ❑ click the **OK** button

   ❑ click the **File** menu

   ❑ click the **Page Setup** menu item

   ❑ click the **Portrait** orientation button

   ❑ click the **OK** button

   Hey, look at that! The script worked perfectly... no surprises. You are now ready to work the exact steps again. Only this time, you will record every click that you make. During the recording process, Captivate creates one screen capture each time that you click your mouse.

Guided Activity 12: Review Recording Settings

1. Show Captivate's Preferences and set the Language and Audio Options.

   ❏ minimize or hide Notepad/TextEdit and return to Captivate (no Captivate projects should be open)

   ❏ if you are using Windows, choose **Edit > Preferences**; if you are using a Mac, choose **Adobe Captivate > Preferences**

   The Preferences dialog box opens. There are three main categories at the left: General Settings, Defaults, and Recording.

   ❏ select the **Recording** category

   ❏ from the **Generate Captions In** drop-down menu, ensure that **English** is selected

Global Preferences: Recording: Settings
Generate Captions In: English ▼

   There are several languages available in the menu, including German, Italian, and Japanese. The language you select controls the text that appears in the Text Captions that are automatically created during the recording process.

   ❏ from the Audio Options area, deselect **Narration**, **System Audio**, **Actions in Real Time**, and **Keystrokes**

   ❏ from the Audio Options area, leave **Camera Sounds** selected

   Audio Options: ☐ Narration   [Audio Settings...]
   ☐ System Audio
   ☐ Actions in Real Time
   ☑ Camera Sounds
   ☐ Keystrokes
   ▨ Hear Keyboard Tap Sounds

   The **Narration** option allows you to record a narrator at the same time that you record the lesson. Because you will not be using audio for the lesson you just rehearsed, you won't need this option. However, this feature could prove useful if you are relying on an SME to both record the lesson and provide the narration. Instead of creating the lesson and the narration on different days, both can be created at the same time. Nevertheless, I typically work with professional audio talent and import audio files into my Captivate projects later during production (you will work with audio on page 145). **System Audio** allows you to record any sounds made by your computer, such as audio associated with a video you are recording or the sound you hear when error messages appear in some applications.

   If you select **Actions in Real Time**, Captivate sets the slide timing for your project slides to match the time it took you to complete a process. If you wait 10 seconds from one click to the next, Captivate sets your slide timing to match. I typically do not use this feature. With **Camera Sounds** selected, you hear a sound effect much like a camera shutter every time Captivate creates a screen capture. If you leave **Keystrokes** selected, Captivate creates an animation within your project that shows what you type, as you're typing—typos and all. I typically do not use this feature. Instead, I allow users to type text

NOTES

NOTES

directly into my Captivate simulations using Text Entry Boxes. You will learn about Text Entry Boxes on page 185.

2. Set the Hide options.

❏ Windows users: from the Hide area, deselect **Recording Window**, **Task Icon**, and **System Tray Icon** (if necessary); Mac users, deselect **Recording Window** and **Dock Icon** (if necessary)

Hide: ☐ Recording Window	Hide: ☐ Recording Window
☐ Task Icon	☐ Dock Icon
☐ System Tray Icon	

In the images above, the Windows options are shown at the left; the Mac options, at the right.

If you had selected **Recording Window**, **Task Icon (Dock Icon)**, and **System Tray Icon**, you would hide all evidence of Captivate during the capture process. These items could get in the way if you were capturing your desktop and the Captivate application icon was on the screen. Because I tend to create software simulations within specific application windows, I typically leave these options deselected.

3. Ensure that new windows always appear in the Recording Area.

❏ from the Others area, ensure **Move New Windows Inside Recording Area** is selected

The **Move New Windows Inside Recording Area** option could prove useful if a window tries to appear outside of the Recording Area. Captivate moves the window into the Recording Area for you. Without this feature, you would have to pause the movie, drag the window into the Recording Area, and continue. I typically enable this feature.

4. Enable Video recording.

❏ from the **Smoothen movements for** area, ensure both **Drag and Drop actions** and **Mouse Wheel Actions** are selected

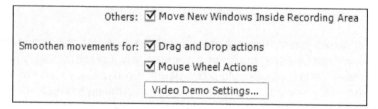

These final two options deal with Video recordings, which you will learn about later.

5. Customize a recording key.

❏ from the **Recording** category at the left, select **Keys - (Global)**

❏ click in the **To Stop Recording** field and press the [y] key on your keyboard

The letter [y] replaces the key that was in the field by default.

To Stop Recording: Y

If you were to move forward and record a lesson using Captivate, you would press **[y]** on your keyboard to end the recording process. You can customize the fields in this dialog box to suit your needs. For most people, the default keys work wonderfully.

6. Reset the default Recording Keys.

   ☐ still in the **Keys - (Global)** area, click the **Restore Defaults** button

   Restore Defaults

   Note: If you're using a Mac, the default **To Stop Recording** shortcut keys **[Cmd] [Enter]** won't work unless you have an extended keyboard. On my Mac, I changed the keyboard shortcut to **[control] [e]** and things work perfectly every time. If you're using a PC and you don't have an End key, you can also elect to use custom keys instead of the default.

   ☐ click the **OK** button

   When clicking the OK button, you might see the alert dialog box below.

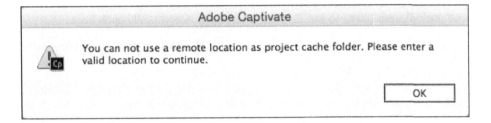

Project Cache is listed among the **General Settings** Preferences. Much like temporary Internet files created by web browsers as you surf the web, the Project Cache folder stores components of all of your projects until you click the **Clear Cache** button. The cached projects make the process of re-opening, saving, and working on projects faster than previous versions of Captivate. However, the Cache folder cannot be located on a remote location, such as a network or external drive. To resolve the issue presented in the dialog box above, select **General Settings** from the **Preferences** category list at the left. From the **Project Cache** area, click the **Browse** button. Open your Local Disk and either select a folder on the disk or create a new one. (I typically create a new folder called **CpCache** directly within My Document (PC) or Document (Mac), but you can use any folder on your local disk). Once you've specified a local location for the cache, you should be able to click the **OK** button to close the Preferences dialog box.

Multimode Recordings

As first mentioned on page 40, there are multiple Automatic recording modes: Demonstration, Assessment Simulation, Training Simulation, and Custom. Each mode is covered during this module.

Demonstration mode is ideal if you want to show a quick software concept to someone, but you don't expect the person to follow along and actually perform the steps being demonstrated. When recording using Demonstration mode, Captivate automatically includes Text Captions (text bubbles that tell users what's happening on the screen), Highlight Boxes (colorful boxes), and a simulated mouse cursor that work together to grab the learner's attention.

Assessment simulations allow you to record and create interactive eLearning at one time. An Assessment includes Click Boxes (to make the lesson interactive) and Failure Captions (to help the user who clicks in the wrong place or performs the wrong step) by default. However, because an Assessment Simulation won't include Text Captions, an Assessment Simulation works best when teamed with a Demonstration. You've likely experienced this kind of eLearning: there's a "show me" lesson that demonstrates a concept; then there's an interactive "let me try" version of the same lesson that is interactive.

Training simulations are similar to Assessments. However, in addition to Click Boxes and Failure Captions being automatically added, you will also gain **Hint Captions** (captions that appear if the learner moves their mouse close to the Click Box but does not actually click anywhere).

Custom recordings can be set up to be a combination of the Demonstration, Assessment, and Training modes.

During the activities that follow, you will review Captivate's default preferences for recording Demonstrations, Assessment simulations, and Training simulations. Then you will use all three modes—at the same time—to record the process of changing the page orientation in Notepad or TextEdit (using the script you rehearsed on page 42).

Guided Activity 13: Review Recording Modes

1. Ensure that Captivate is still running (no projects should be open).

2. Display Captivate's Preferences dialog box.

   ☐ if you are using Windows, choose **Edit > Preferences**; if you are using a Mac, choose **Adobe Captivate > Preferences**

3. Review the default settings for Demonstration mode.

   ☐ from the **Recording** categories at the left, select **Modes**

   Notice that there is a Mode drop-down menu at the right.

   ☐ from the **Mode** drop-down menu, choose **Demonstration**

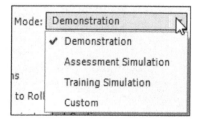

❏ from the bottom of the dialog box, click the **Restore Defaults** button

It's possible that clicking the Restore Defaults button didn't do anything to the settings you see on your screen. However, clicking the button has reset the options to Captivate's original settings. Because I have no idea if you (or someone else) has changed the recording settings, it's a good idea to restore the defaults. At this point, the settings are back to what you would see after starting Captivate for the first time. After you have completed the lessons in this module, you can modify the recording settings.

❏ review the **Captions** area

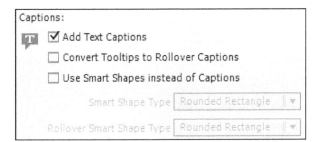

In the Captions area, notice that **Add Text Captions** is selected by default. **Convert Tooltips to Rollover Captions** and **Use Smart Shapes instead of Captions** are both deselected. You will learn how to insert and work with Text Captions beginning on page 86. During the recording process, Captivate creates Text Captions for you, which is, quite frankly, awesome. You learned how to work with Smart Shapes on page 34 and you'll learn about Rollover Captions on page 142. Once you are more comfortable with Captivate you can come back to this dialog box and experiment with what those two options do for your screen recordings. For now, leave both options deselected.

❏ review the **Mouse** area

In the Mouse area, notice that **Show Mouse Location and Movement** and **Add Highlight Boxes on Click** are both selected by default. By including the Mouse Location, learners see a mouse move around the screen as they watch your demonstration. The mouse they see is actually mimicking where you pointed and clicked during the recording process. And by adding Highlight Boxes, learners see a colorful box that leads the eye to the area of the screen where the action is occurring. You will learn how to modify several aspects of the mouse pointer beginning on page 108; you will learn how to work with Highlight Boxes on page 114.

❏ review the **Click Boxes** area

NOTES

NOTES

In the Click Boxes area, notice that none of the options are selected... nor can you select them. Click Boxes add interactivity to your eLearning lessons. They're great, but because demonstrations are not interactive, you don't need Click Boxes. The other modes (which you will review next) rely heavily on Click Boxes. (You will learn how to add Click Boxes to a project manually beginning on page 181.)

❑ review the **Text Entry Boxes** area

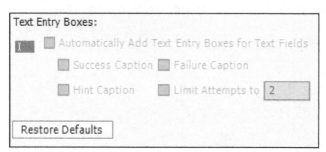

As with Click Boxes, Text Entry Boxes are deselected by default. Text Entry Boxes are also interactive and allow learners to type directly within a simulation. (You will learn how to add Text Entry Boxes to a project beginning on page 185.)

4. Review the default settings for Assessment Simulation mode.

❑ from the **Mode** drop-down menu, choose **Assessment Simulation**

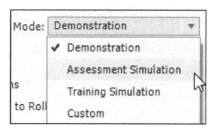

❑ from the bottom of the dialog box, click the **Restore Defaults** button

❑ review the **Captions** area

Because learners who take this lesson are expected to prove that they understand the demonstration they likely watched before opening the assessment, there isn't a need to include text captions. For that reason, the captions are disabled by default.

❑ review the **Mouse** area

Because this lesson is interactive, allowing Captivate to create an artificial mouse would be confusing to the learner. Both the Mouse and Highlight Box options are disabled by default.

☐ review the **Click Boxes** and **Text Entry Boxes** areas

> Click Boxes:
> ☑ Add Click Boxes on Mouse Click
> ☐ Success Caption ☑ Failure Caption
> ☐ Hint Caption ☐ Limit Attempts to 2
> ☐ Show Hand Cursor on the Click Box
>
> Text Entry Boxes:
> ☑ Automatically Add Text Entry Boxes for Text Fields
> ☐ Success Caption ☑ Failure Caption
> ☐ Hint Caption ☐ Limit Attempts to 2

An Assessment Simulation is expected to be interactive. Both Click Boxes and Text Entry Boxes are selected by default. In addition, Failure Caption is enabled. If the learner clicks in the wrong place while moving through the lesson, the learner sees a correction via the Failure Caption.

5. Review the default settings for Training Simulation mode.

☐ from the **Mode** drop-down menu, choose **Training Simulation**

☐ from the bottom of the dialog box, click the **Restore Defaults** button

☐ review the **Captions** and **Mouse** areas

As with the Assessment Simulation, there is no need for captions, the mouse, or Highlight Boxes.

☐ review the **Click Boxes** and **Text Entry Boxes** areas

As with the Assessment Simulation, a lesson created using this mode is expected to be interactive. Both Click Boxes and Text Entry Boxes are selected by default (along with Failure Captions). Notice that **Hint Caption** is also selected. If the learner gets close to the location of the Click Box, the learner gets a hint about how to proceed. Hint Captions are great if your learner doesn't have strong mouse skills, tends to point at screen objects, but doesn't naturally click the mouse.

> ☑ Hint Caption

6. Close the Preferences dialog box by clicking the **OK** button.

Note to Mac Users: You're about to record screen actions. However, if you are using two monitors, it's possible that you won't see the red Captivate Recording Area shown on the next page. I've been able to get the recording area to appear by choosing **Apple > System Preferences > Displays > Arrangement** and selecting **Mirror Displays**. Although you won't be able to take advantage of having multiple monitors while recording screen actions using Captivate, you can turn off Mirror Displays once the recording process is complete.

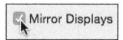

Guided Activity 14: Record a Simulation Using Multiple Modes

1. Ensure that Captivate is running (no projects should be open).

2. Ensure that Notepad or TextEdit is running (see page 42).

3. Display the Recording Area and control panel.

   ❏ from within Captivate, click the **New** tab on the Home screen

   ❏ double-click **Software Simulation** (or choose **File > Record new Software Simulation**)

   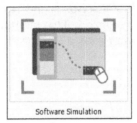

   Notice that there is a red box. Known as the Recording Area, this is the area of the screen that will be captured during the recording process. There is also a control panel containing Size and Recording Type controls.

   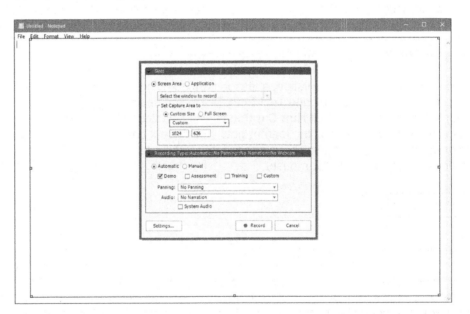

   When recording, consider using the smallest Recording Area that works for you and your particular application. The smaller the Recording Area, the fewer pixels you are capturing and the fewer megabytes you published project will be. The fewer the megabytes, the faster your learners can download and consume your eLearning content. (Published project sizes become particularly important if your learner's Internet access is slow or limited. When possible, fewer megabytes are better.)

4. Specify what Captivate is supposed to record.

WINDOWS USERS (Mac users, your instructions are half a page further down)**:**

☐ from the top of the control panel, select **Application**

☐ from the **Select the window to record** drop-down menu that appears, select **Untitled - Notepad**

On your screen, notice that the red Recording Area and Notepad occupy the same space. By specifying Notepad as the Application, Captivate's Recording Area is now focusing on Notepad

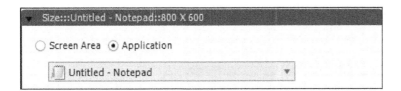

☐ from the **Snap to** area, select **Custom Size**

☐ select **800 x 600** from the drop-down menu

The Recording Area resizes to 800 x 600. And because you selected Application, the Notepad application also resizes to 800 x 600.

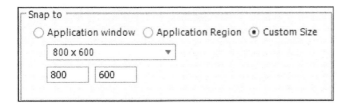

The next few steps are for Mac users only. Windows users, skip to **step 5** below. (Look for the text ALL USERS.)

MAC USERS:

The menu bar in your applications stays locked at the top of the screen (the menu does not float in the application's window like Windows applications). You won't typically use the **Application** or **Snap To** selections unless the process you are recording does not include the menu bar. During the following recording process, you will be including the menu bar as you change the Page Orientation within TextEdit. You need to manually specify a Screen Area for Captivate to record.

☐ from the top of the control panel, select **Screen Area**

☐ ensure the **Set Capture Area to** is set to **Custom Size**

☐ select **800 x 600** from the drop-down menu

❏ drag and resize the **TextEdit** window and red **Recording Area** as necessary until your screen looks similar to the image below (notice that the TextEdit menu bar is within the Recording Area)

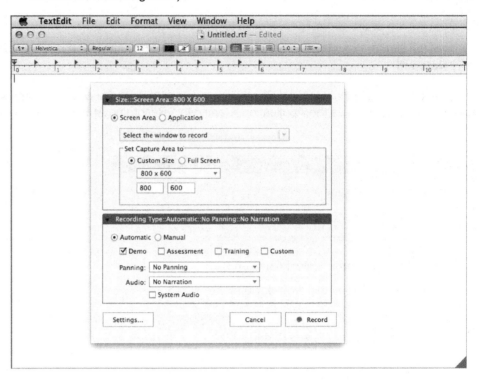

ALL USERS:

5. Select a Recording Mode.

❏ from the **Recording Type** area of the Control panel, select **Automatic**

With this option selected, every click of your mouse during the recording process creates a screen capture. In contrast, had you selected **Manual** mode, you would need to press a key on your keyboard (typically the [**print screen**] key for Windows users, [**command**] [**F6**] for Mac users) to capture the screen.

❏ select **Demo**, **Assessment**, and **Training** from the list of modes

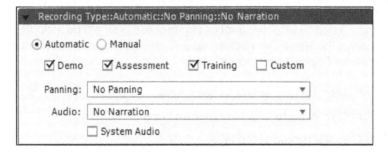

6. Disable Panning and Audio Narration.

☐ ensure that Panning is set to **No Panning** and that Audio is set to **No Narration**

☐ if necessary, deselect **System Audio**

You'll learn about Panning later (page 60). Although audio is a good thing in your eLearning, in my experience, it is best to create the audio later (during production). You will learn to work with audio beginning on page 141.

7. Record multiple modes.

☐ click the **Record** button

You see a 3-second countdown and then nothing.

While nothing seems to have happened, Captivate is waiting patiently for you to follow your script, and click within either Notepad or TextEdit.

☐ using your mouse, click the **File** menu within Notepad or TextEdit

☐ click the **Page Setup** menu item

☐ from the **Orientation** area, click **Landscape**

☐ click the **OK** button

☐ click the **File** menu

☐ click the **Page Setup** menu item

☐ click the **Portrait** orientation button and then click the **OK** button

8. Stop the recording.

☐ **Windows users**, press [**end**] on your keyboard; **Mac users**, press [**control**] [**e**] (or whatever stop recording shortcut you set up) on your keyboard

Once you stop the recording process, slides are created and three unsaved projects open in Captivate.

Note: If you cannot get Captivate to stop recording via your keyboard shortcut, you can manually stop the recording process by clicking the Captivate icon in the **Task Bar/System Tray** (Windows users) or the **Dock** (Mac users).

9. Preview the demo.

☐ near the top of the Captivate window, notice that there are three tabs, one untitled project for each mode you selected prior to recording

| untitled_demo1.cptx ✕ | untitled_assessment1.cptx ✕ | untitled_training1.cptx ✕ |

NOTES

□ select the first tab (**untitled_demo1**)

□ from the toolbar, click **Preview** and choose **Project**

As the preview plays, notice that the project contains text captions and Highlight Boxes. You will learn how to create captions from scratch as you move through the lessons in this book. If this is your first time automatically recording an eLearning project, there is a good chance you have just been blown away with the fact that Captivate added reasonable, usable text to your new lesson out of the box. *Very cool!*

Note to Mac users: If you didn't get any text captions during the recording process or you received an error message while trying to record, try this: Close but don't save any open projects. Click the **Apple** menu and choose **System Preferences**. Select **Security & Privacy**. Select **Accessibility** and then, from the **Allow the apps below to control your computer** area, select **Adobe Captivate.app**. Close the window and then try recording again.

10. When the preview is finished, close the preview by pressing the [**Esc**] key on your keyboard.

11. Close the demo project (there is no need to save it).

    Two projects should still be open: **untitled_assessment** and **untitled_training**.

Preview Confidence Check

1. Preview the **untitled_assessment** project. As you do, notice that using this mode has created an interactive simulation. You can click where you were supposed to click to move to the next slide and continue the lesson. Click anywhere else on the screen to see a Failure Caption.

2. When finished with the **untitled_assessment** project, close it without saving it.

3. Preview the **untitled_training** project. As you do, notice that using this lesson is nearly identical to the assessment lesson you just closed. However, when you move your mouse close to the area of the screen where you are supposed to click, you see the Hint Captions.

    You've got to admit that this is awesome stuff... three modes, three projects... and all it took you was a few clicks here and there.

4. When finished with the **untitled_training** project, close it without saving it.

Custom Recordings

You have now learned how to record three kinds of eLearning lessons with Adobe Captivate: Demonstrations, Assessment Simulations, and Training Simulations. Between demonstrations and simulations, which type of lesson results in the most effective learning experience for your users? There is no clear-cut answer.

Demonstrations are relatively quick and easy to create (you just did). However, demonstrations do not allow for learner interaction. When learners watch a demonstration rather than participate in an interactive simulation, the potential for learning is reduced. The Text Captions that are automatically created by Captivate are great, but they are written in the imperative, or command, form. For instance, a typical Text Caption created by Captivate is likely to say something like "Select the File Menu." Upon reading that instruction, a learner is likely to take the caption's instructions literally and attempt to select the File menu. Unfortunately, at the same time that the learner is trying to interact with the demonstration, a mouse pointer that Captivate created when the lesson was recorded is likely moving around the screen. In this case, you're going to end up with one confused and possibly frustrated learner.

Simulations are perfect for assessing what a learner has absorbed during a demonstration. However, because Simulations do not add any Text Captions by default, there are no instructions telling learners what to do. Learners either perform the required steps or click incorrectly somewhere on the screen and see a Failure Caption. Some people consider this kind of approach to eLearning to be a bit harsh because the learner is often experiencing negative feedback with no guidance.

Many Captivate developers create both a Demonstration and a Simulation. That's all well and good until you remember that it could take several hours to produce the lessons. If you elect to produce both a Demonstration and an Assessment, you are essentially making twice the work for yourself.

Demonstration or Simulation: Which Mode is Best?

Instead of creating a Demonstration and a Simulation, I recommend you record a custom, or hybrid, lesson that incorporates the best of the Demonstration, Assessment, and Training modes.

When you are finished recording the custom lesson, the result is a lesson that bridges the gap between a Demonstration and an Assessment/Simulation lesson.

Guided Activity 15: Record a Custom Simulation

1. Set the Preferences for the simulation you are about to record.

   ☐ Windows users, choose **Edit > Preferences**;
   Mac users, choose **Adobe Captivate > Preferences**

   ☐ from the **Recording** category, select **Modes**

   ☐ from the Mode drop-down menu, select **Custom**

Mode:	Custom ▾

   ☐ click the **Restore Defaults** button at the bottom of the dialog box

   ☐ from the Captions area, select **Add Text Captions**

   Captions:
   ☑ Add Text Captions
   ☐ Convert Tooltips to Rollover Captions
   ☐ Use Smart Shapes instead of Captions
   Smart Shape Type | Rounded Rectangle ▾
   Rollover Smart Shape Type | Rounded Rectangle ▾

   ☐ from the Click Boxes area, select **Add Click Boxes on Mouse Click** and **Failure Caption**

   Click Boxes:
   ☑ Add Click Boxes on Mouse Click
   ☐ Success Caption ☑ Failure Caption
   ☐ Hint Caption   ☐ Limit Attempts to [2]
   ☐ Show Hand Cursor on the Click Box

   By now you should be somewhat comfortable with the available options in this dialog box. You have selected **Add Text Captions** so that the Text Captions are created for you (like you saw with a Demonstration). *Nice.* And because the captions are written in the imperative, you may be able to use them in the new lesson with little editing. *Nicer.* Everything else has been left deselected except for **Click Boxes** and **Failure Caption** (like the simulation modes). These two settings result in a highly interactive simulation out of the box. *Nicest!*

   ☐ click the **OK** button

2. Record the custom simulation.

☐ from within Captivate, click the **New** tab on the Home screen

☐ double-click **Software Simulation** (or choose **File > Record new Software Simulation**)

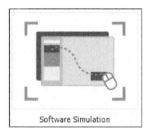

Captivate once again hides, and the recording options appear. Notice that the settings you specified last were remembered so you don't have to set the Screen Area options again (if you closed Notepad or TextEdit, you can review the Screen Area settings on page 50).

3. Record the Custom simulation.

☐ ensure that you're still capturing either the **Notepad** application or **TextEdit** screen area

☐ from the **Recording Type** area, select **Custom**

☐ deselect the other modes

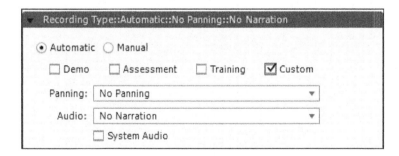

☐ click the **Record** button and, once the Countdown goes away, use your mouse to click the **File** menu within Notepad or TextEdit

☐ click the **Page Setup** menu item

☐ from the **Orientation** area, click **Landscape**

☐ click the **OK** button

☐ click the **File** menu

☐ click the **Page Setup** menu item

☐ click the **Portrait** orientation button

☐ click the **OK** button

NOTES

4. Stop the recording process.

5. Preview the project.

   As you move through the lesson, notice that the Text Captions are written in the imperative to encourage interactivity. There may be one or two captions you need to edit (some of the buttons are likely mislabeled, especially on the Mac side). Nevertheless, much of the caption-writing work is done.

   Also notice that there are Click Boxes (hot spots) that make this lesson 100 percent interactive.

6. When finished previewing the lesson, close the preview.

7. Close the project (there is no need to save it).

Recording Confidence Check

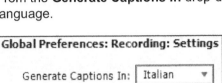

Record a lesson using caption written in a language other than English:

1. Display the Preferences dialog box (Edit menu for Windows users; Adobe Captivate menu for Mac users).

2. From the categories at the left, select **Recording**.

3. From the **Generate Captions In** drop-down menu, choose any language.

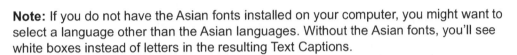

Global Preferences: Recording: Settings
Generate Captions In: Italian ▼

Note: If you do not have the Asian fonts installed on your computer, you might want to select a language other than the Asian languages. Without the Asian fonts, you'll see white boxes instead of letters in the resulting Text Captions.

4. Create another Software Simulation with Notepad or TextEdit that uses the Custom mode. (When you record the simulation, run through the same script you have used throughout this module).

5. Stop the recording process and preview the project.

Notice that the Text Captions are using the language you specified in the **Generate Captions In** drop-down menu.

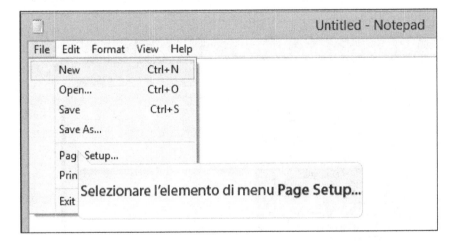

6. Close the project (there is no need to save it when prompted).

7. Display the **Preferences** dialog box again and set the Recording language back to English.

8. Close Notepad/TextEdit (there is no need to save if prompted).

NOTES

Panning

Captivate's Panning feature is useful when you want to record something on your computer that is outside of the red Recording Area. If you enable Panning prior to recording and use Captivate's Automatic mode, clicking outside of the Recording Area forces Captivate to move the Recording Area and includes the area you clicked. You can also use Manual Panning where you drag the Recording Area to the area of the screen you would like to record.

Guided Activity 16: Record a Demonstration that Pans

1. Start a web browser and navigate to **www.disney.com**.

2. Switch to Captivate and create a new Software Simulation.

3. Select a screen area to record instead of a specific application.

   ☐ from the top of the control panel, select **Screen Area**

4. Specify a recording size.

   ☐ from the Set Capture Area to area, select **Custom Size**

   ☐ from the next drop-down menu, select **640 x 480**

5. Drag the red recording box to the **upper left** of the browser window.

6. Resize the browser window so it's about 40 percent larger than the red Recording Area.

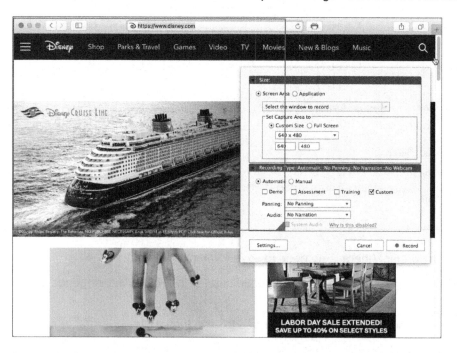

Because you selected Screen Area instead of Application, the red Recording Area stays sized to 640 x 480 and does not get larger as you resize the browser window.

More important, there are areas on the Disney site that are not within the red recording area. If you record and click outside of the recording area, none of those actions will be recorded or seen by learners. This is a perfect place to use the Panning feature.

---

7. Select a Recording Mode.

   ☐ from the Recording Type area of the Control panel, ensure **Automatic** is selected

   ☐ from the list of modes, select **Demo** and then **deselect** the other modes

8. Enable Panning.

   ☐ from the **Panning** drop-down menu, choose **Manual Panning**

   ◉ Automatic ○ Manual

      ☑ Demo   ☐ Assessment   ☐ Training   ☐ Custom

   Panning: Manual Panning   ▼

   Audio: No Narration   ▼

           ☐ System Audio

9. Record the Demo.

   ☐ click the **Record** button

   ☐ click one or two of the menus on the Disney website (within the red Recording Area)

10. Manually pan.

    ☐ **carefully drag** the right edge of the red Recording Area **right** so some of the menus at the right of the Disney website are within the Recording Area

    ☐ click one of the Disney website menus within the recording area

11. Stop the recording process.

12. Preview the project to see the panning feature in action.

13. When finished previewing the project, close the preview.

14. Save the new project to the **Captivate2019Data** folder as **ExampleOfPanning**.

15. Close the project.

Panning Confidence Check

1. Record the Disney software demo you just worked through one more time with **Automatic** panning.

2. When finished recording, preview the project.

3. When finished previewing the project, close the preview.

4. Close the project without saving.

Manual Recordings

If you've stepped through all of the activities in this module, you've now used every recording option in Captivate except two—Manual mode and Video mode. In most instances, recording screen actions using Captivate's Automatic Recording type gets the job done for you. However, you will come across some applications where attempting to record automatically does not work (some applications won't get along with Captivate and prove difficult to record). This is a perfect opportunity to use Captivate's Manual recording type.

> **Note:** If you are running a screen capture utility (such as SnagIt), disable or close it prior to trying to record manually with Captivate. If a competing screen capture application is running, that program will grab screen captures instead of Captivate.

Guided Activity 17: Manually Record the Screen

1. Ensure that Captivate is still running (no projects should be open).

2. Rehearse the lesson you are going to record.

   ☐ return to the Disney website: **www.disney.com**

   ☐ point, but don't click on some of the links on the Disney site

   You'd like to capture the process of pointing to site objects, but recording the action with Captivate is going to be difficult because it takes mouse clicks to create screen captures.

3. Display the recording control panel.

   ☐ return to Captivate and create a new **Software Simulation**

4. Select the Disney site as the Application to record.

   ☐ from the top of the control panel, select **Application**

   ☐ from the Select window drop-down menu, choose the Disney site

   ☐ from the Snap to area, select **Custom Size**

   ☐ from the next drop-down menu, choose **640 x 480** (if necessary)

5. Select the Manual Recording Type.

☐ from the Recording Type area of the Control panel, select **Manual**

☐ change the Panning to **No Panning**

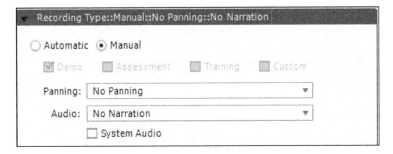

6. Record the Manual Demo.

☐ click the **Record** button

Unlike the other modes, no screen capture is created for you. You'll need to create every screen capture on your own.

☐ **Windows users**, press [**Print Screen**] on your keyboard (depending on your systems configuration, you might have to press [**Fn**] [**Print Screen**]);
Mac users, press [**Command**] [**F6**]

☐ point to one of the links on the navigation bar

☐ **Windows users**, press [**Print Screen**] on your keyboard;
Mac users, press [**Command**] [**F6**]

☐ point to another one of the links on the navigation bar

☐ **Windows users**, press [**Print Screen**] on your keyboard;
Mac users, press [**Command**] [**F6**]

Note: Mac users may find it tough, if not impossible, to use the function keys to create manual shots because those keys might activate special features (those special features are printed on each key). You can disable the special features by displaying the Mac's **System Preferences** (via the Apple menu) and selecting **Keyboard**. On the **Keyboard** tab, select **Use all F1, F2, etc. keys as standard function keys**. Alternatively, you can display the **Keys - Global** Preference within Captivate and change the Manual Recording Key.

> ☑ Use all F1, F2, etc. keys as standard function keys
> When this option is selected, press the Fn key to use the special features printed on each key.

7. Stop the recording.

8. Preview the project, and notice that the screens you captured appear. But this is a bare-bones recording. You would now need to move through the project and add required project assets that recording in the Automatic mode would normally have included (Text Captions, Highlight Boxes, etc.).

9. Close the project (there is no need to save it).

Notes

iCONLOGiC

"Skills and Drills" Learning

Module 4: Video Demos

In This Module You Will Learn About:

And You Will Learn To:

Recording Video Demos

When you record a Software Simulation using one of Captivate's automatic recording modes (such as the Custom mode you used on page 55), mouse clicks result in screen captures. However, if you want to quickly create a software demonstration, you can record a Video Demo. When you record a Video Demo, instead of creating individual slides for mouse clicks, Captivate creates one seamless video.

Video Demos are easier and faster to produce than Software Simulations because the editing capabilities of a Video Demo are more limited than what you find within a standard Captivate project. In a standard project, you edit one slide at a time, each slide has its own Timeline, and there are few limits to what you can add to a slide. In a Video Demo, there aren't any individual slides (there's no Filmstrip at all). There's a Timeline, but just one... and it contains the entire video. You can add several standard Captivate objects to a Video Demo including text captions, highlight boxes, smart shapes, images, animations, and Characters. However, you cannot add interactivity or quizzes to Video Demos (say goodbye to such interactive favorites as click boxes, learner interactions, buttons, and text entry boxes). While you cannot import standard Captivate projects into a Video Demo project, you can import a Video Demo project into a standard Captivate project (via **Insert > CPVC Slide**).

Guided Activity 18: Record a Video Demo

1. Ensure that Captivate is running (no projects need to be open).

2. Set Captivate's Video Demo Preferences.

   ☐ Windows users, choose **Edit > Preferences**;
   Mac users, choose **Adobe Captivate > Preferences**

   ☐ from the **Recording** category, click **Video Demo**

   ☐ ensure that your options match the picture below (with the exception of the Working Folder because the information in that field varies from computer to computer and platform to platform)

Global Recording: Video Demo Recording

☑ Show Mouse in Video Demo Mode

Working Folder: | C:\Users\Administrator\AppData\Local\Temp\CP | Browse... |

Video Color Mode:

○ 16 bit   ⦿ 32 bit

Note: 32-bit mode produces videos with higher quality and larger size.

By selecting **Show Mouse in Video Demo Mode**, the video you record will include your mouse pointer in the resulting video.

Videos created using **32 bit mode** typically result in a larger video when compared to 16 bit videos. Although larger in file size than 16 bit videos, they'll look awesome. As you become more comfortable recording in Video Mode, experiment with the quality you get using both options. In the end, you should use the option that yields the best results for you.

   ☐ click the **OK** button

Note: You are about to use your web browser to visit the Disney site. The Disney home page may feature videos complete with music and other loud sound effects. If you are in an office setting, consider lowering the volume on your computer before going on the next step.

3. Rehearse the lesson you are going to record.

   ❏ switch to your web browser and, if necessary, return to the **Disney** website (**www.disney.com**)

   Like many commercial websites, the Disney home page is very long. You will not be able to use Captivate to capture the entire length of the page using standard screen captures. Instead, you will record a Video Demo that captures everything you do as you scroll around the Disney home page.

   ❏ at the right side of the browser window, drag the scroll bar **down** a few inches and then release your mouse

   ❏ drag the scroll bar **down** another few inches and then release your mouse

   ❏ drag the scroll back to the top of the page

   And that's it. At this point, you will stop the recording process. Let's return to Captivate and record the same actions using Video Mode.

4. Display the recording control panel.

   ❏ switch back to Captivate

   ❏ choose **File > Record a new > Video Demo**

   Just like recording a Software Simulation, the main Captivate interface hides and the recording features open.

5. Select the browser window as the Application.

   ❏ from the top of the control panel, select **Application**

   ❏ from the drop-down menu that appears beneath Application, select the browser application you used to go to the Disney website

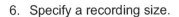

6. Specify a recording size.

   ❏ from the **Snap to** area, select **Custom Size**

   ❏ from the next drop-down menu, select **1024 x 576**

7. Disable Panning, Audio, and the Webcam.

   ☐ ensure that **Panning** is set to **No Panning**

   ☐ ensure that **Audio** is set to **No Narration**

   ☐ from the Webcam drop-down menu, choose **No Webcam**

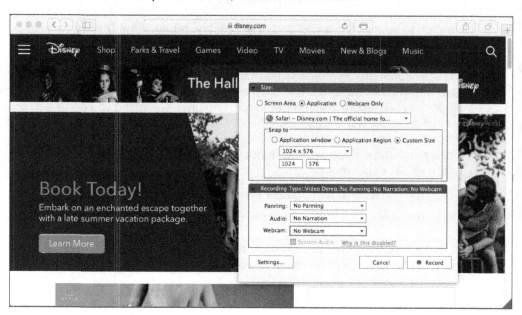

8. Record the Video Demo.

   ☐ click the **Record** button and wait for the countdown to go away

   ☐ at the right side of the browser window, drag the scroll bar **down** a few inches, and then release your mouse

   ☐ drag the scroll bar **down** another few inches and then release your mouse

   ☐ drag the scroll back to the top of the page

9. Stop the recording process and preview the video.

   Note: As mentioned during the previous module, if you can't get Captivate to stop recording via your keyboard shortcut, you can always manually stop the recording process by clicking the Captivate icon in the Task Bar/System Tray (Windows users) or the Dock (Mac users).

Once you stop the Recording process, you are returned to Captivate, and the lesson automatically plays within a Full Screen Preview. If you are a seasoned Captivate developer, you will find this behavior a bit strange. When you end the recording process in every other Captivate recording mode, you are taken into Captivate's main interface where you would produce the lesson. You could preview the lesson at regular intervals along the way, but previewing is a process you need to initiate. With Video Demos, the first thing you do is preview the recording and then edit the video as needed.

10. Enter Video Edit mode.

   ❏ from the lower, right of the Preview window, click the **Edit** button

Once again, if you've spent any amount of time working within Captivate, things may seem a bit strange. For instance, there isn't a Filmstrip at the left. If you click Properties at the far right of the window, you will see that there is a new panel named **Video Effects** that has three tabs (Pan & Zoom, Popup, and Transitions). Notice also that the untitled video has a unique extension. Standard Captivate projects use a **cptx** extension. Video projects contain a **cpvc** extension, which stands for Captivate Video Composition.

11. Save the video project to the **Captivate2019Data** folder as **ScrollingDisney** and then close it. (You can also close the web browser containing the Disney website.)

Zooming and Panning

Captivate's Pan & Zoom feature is really two cool tools in one. Zooming gives you the ability to automatically get the learner closer to the action. Panning lets you automatically change the area of the screen that the learner sees.

Guided Activity 19: Add a Video Zoom

1. Using Captivate, open the **PanZoomMe** video project from the Captivate2019Data folder.

2. Preview the video.

   ☐ choose **Preview > Project**

   This video demonstrates how to change both the Font and the Font Size in Microsoft Notepad. You are going to use the Pan & Zoom feature to move learners closer to the action.

   ☐ press [**esc**] to close the preview

3. Add a Pan & Zoom point to the Timeline.

   ☐ on the Timeline, click on the **2**-second mark

   The Playhead (the red bar) should be lined up at the 2-second mark on the Timeline. This is the part of the video where the Format menu is just about to be clicked.

   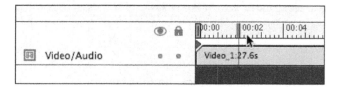

   ☐ choose **Window > Video Effects**

   The Video Effects Inspector opens at the right of the Captivate window. There are three tabs: **Pan & Zoom**, **Popup**, and **Transitions**. (If the Video Effects Inspector is not on your screen, choose **Window > Video Effects** again.)

   ☐ on the **Video Effects** Inspector, select the **Pan & Zoom** tab

   ☐ click the **Add Pan & Zoom** button

   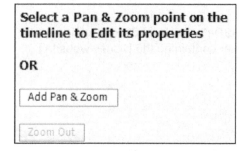

On the Timeline, a Pan & Zoom **marker** has been added (it's the orange circle with a magnifying glass in the middle).

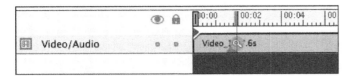

4. Change the Scale of the zoom.

□ on the **Video Effects Inspector**, **Pan & Zoom** tab, change the **Scale** to **125** and press [**enter**]

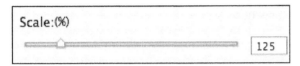

Notice two things. On the slide itself, you are closer to the Notepad menus. On the Pan & Zoom tab, you can see the area targeted by the zoom.

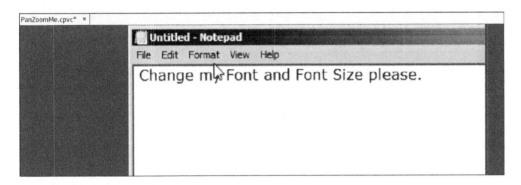

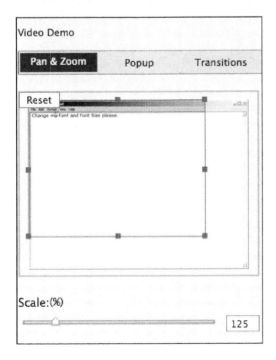

5. On the Timeline, drag the Playhead left to the beginning of the Timeline.

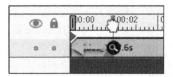

6. Preview the video (Preview > Project).

   At the 2-second mark, you are automatically zoomed closer to Notepad's Format menu. Zooming closer to the action is an awesome feature. But there's a problem. You've zoomed very close to the action. However, you cannot see the font and font size being changed. You'll take care of that problem next by adding a second Pan & Zoom point on the Timeline and Panning across the video.

7. Close the Preview.

   ☐ click the **Edit** button in the lower right of the Preview window

Guided Activity 20: Add a Video Pan

1. Ensure that the **PanZoomMe** video project is still open.

2. Add a second Pan & Zoom point to the Timeline.

   ☐ on the Timeline, click on the **5.7**-second mark

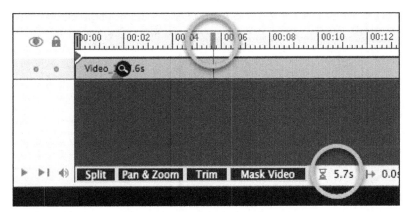

   The Playhead (the red bar) should be lined up at the 5.7-second mark on the Timeline. This is the part of the video where Notepad's Font dialog box opens. You can tell that you've positioned the Playhead at the 5.7-second mark by observing the number at the right of the hourglass icon on the Timeline.

   ☐ on the **Pan & Zoom** tab, click the **Add Pan & Zoom** button

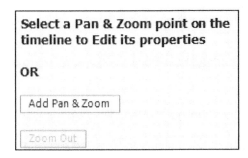

   On the Timeline, notice that a second Pan & Zoom marker has been added.

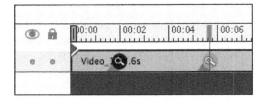

   On the Pan & Zoom tab, notice that the Zoom scale and position is identical to what you created with the first Pan & Zoom marker. As you add more and more points along the Timeline, the new points always retain the attributes of the previous point.

3. Pan the video.

☐ on the **Pan & Zoom** tab, drag the Pan & Zoom area down and to the right so that it is centered over the Font dialog box

By dragging the Pan & Zoom area, you've panned the screen and changed what the learners see when they watch the demo.

☐ on the **Pan & Zoom** tab, resize the Zoom area so that the Font dialog box is within the Pan & Zoom area

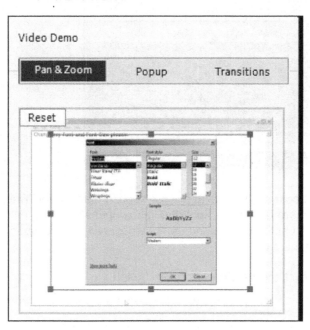

By resizing the Pan & Zoom area, you've changed how close the learners are to the video.

4. Position the Playhead at the beginning of the Timeline and then Preview the video.

At the 2-second mark, you are automatically zoomed closer to Notepad's Format menu. Next you pan right and can see what's happening within the Font dialog box. Awesome!

5. Close the Preview (by clicking the Edit button).

Note: You can remove a Pan & Zoom point from the Timeline at any time by right-clicking the point and choosing **Remove Pan & Zoom**. And you can change the attributes of any Pan & Zoom by selecting the Pan & Zoom point on the Timeline and editing the options as appropriate via the Pan & Zoom tab.

Pan & Zoom Confidence Check

1. Ensure that the **PanZoomMe** video project is still open.

2. On the Timeline, click at the **25.4**-second mark. (This is where the OK button is clicked in the Font dialog box.)

3. On the Pan & Zoom tab, click the **Zoom Out** button to instantly resize the Zoom Area (so that learners can see the entire Notepad window).

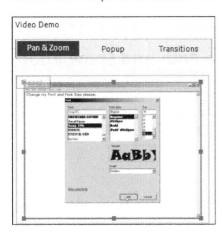

4. Preview from the beginning of the video to see the three Pan & Zooms that have been added to the video.

    Now you'll get a chance to add a transition to the beginning and end of the video.

5. On the left of the Timeline, select the **icon** that looks like one-half of a diamond. (This is one of two Transition Markers you have in the video... the other marker is on the right side of the Timeline.)

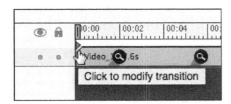

    On the Video Effects Inspector, notice that there is a **Transitions** tab.

6. Select any of the Transitions that you like; then click the half diamond at the right and add a Transition to the end of the video.

7. At the right of the Timeline, drag the **yellow rectangle** a bit to the right to extend the playtime for the video by a second or so.

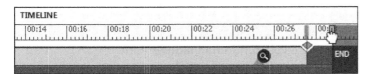

8. Preview from the beginning of the video to see the new Transition effects.

9. Save your work. Keep the project open for the next activity.

Mouse Points

If you had recorded a software Demonstration, the project you created would have included a mouse pointer on every slide that can easily be edited (the pointer can be moved or deleted, and its appearance changed). Unfortunately, the project you are working with is a video. You can see the mouse pointer moving around the screen, but you cannot edit it. Or can you? Although it is not obvious that you have any mouse editing features in a Video Demo, looks are deceiving. In fact, you can display the mouse points within a Video Demo and perform such feats as deleting a mouse point, changing the appearance of the mouse, smoothing out the mouse path, and adding visual mouse clicks.

Guided Activity 21: Smooth a Mouse Path and Show Visual Clicks

1. Ensure that the **PanZoomMe** video project is still open.

2. Display the Mouse Points.

   ☐ choose **Edit > Edit Mouse Points**

   On the Timeline, several mouse points appear. Each of the mouse points can be selected and edited.

   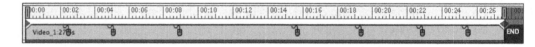

3. Smoothen a Mouse Path.

   ☐ on the **Timeline**, select the **first mouse point**

   On the video, notice that the mouse path begins in the middle of the screen and moves to the Format menu. The path taken by the mouse isn't as smooth as it could be. You'll fix that next.

   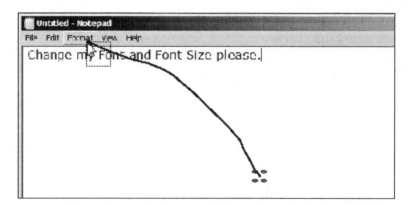

   ☐ on the Properties Inspector, select **Smoothen Mouse Path**

   ☑ *Smoothen Mouse Path

On the screen, notice that the appearance of the mouse path has gone from a jagged path to a smooth curve.

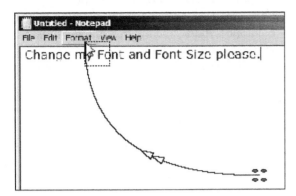

4. Show the Mouse Click.

   ☐ with the first mouse point still selected, select **Show Mouse Click** from the Properties Inspector

   ☐ from the drop-down menu below **Show Mouse Click**, choose **Custom**

   ☐ from the next drop-down menu, choose any of the animations (you can preview the animation by clicking the Play button to the right of the drop-down menu)

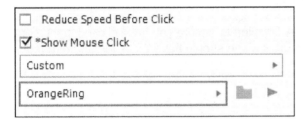

5. Preview from the beginning of the video to see the new mouse path and visual click.

6. Save and close the project.

Splitting

You have now learned how to create a Video Demo (page 66), how to use Pan and Zoom (page 70), and how to add Transitions (page 75). One limitation of Transitions is that you can add a Transition only to Transition Markers (the diamonds you see at the beginning and end of every video). But what if you need to add a Transition to the middle of a video segment? That's the perfect case for Splitting a single video into multiple pieces.

Guided Activity 22: Split a Video

1. Open the **SplitMe** video project from the Captivate2019Data folder.

2. Preview the Project.

    This video demonstrates two Notepad concepts: how to cut and paste text and how to change the Font and Font Size of text. Your goal is to add a transition between the first and second parts of the lesson. (Transitions have already been added to the beginning and end of the video.)

    ☐ click the **Edit** button to close the preview

3. Split the video into two segments.

    ☐ on the Timeline, click on the **25.0**-second mark

    Once again, use the bottom of the Timeline to ensure you have clicked in the correct part of the Timeline. The hour glass icon you see should have 25.0s just to the right.

    ☐ on the bottom left of the Timeline, click the **Split** button

    On the Timeline, notice that the video has been split into two segments and that there is a Transition Marker between the two segments.

Transitions Confidence Check

1. Ensure that the **SplitMe** video project is still open.

2. Add any Transition you like to the new Transition Marker. Need help? See page 75.

3. Preview the video from the beginning to see the new Transition effect.

4. Save and close the project.

Trimming

During the recording process, every recording misstep or delay shows up in a Video Demo. For instance, if you intend to show the process of accessing the File menu in an application and accidentally open a different menu, the gaffe is recorded. The same is true if you begin the recording process but take several seconds to move your mouse. Every second and everything you do is being recorded. If you've recorded some missteps, you'll find the Trim feature in Captivate invaluable.

Guided Activity 23: Trim a Video

1. Open the **TrimMe** video project from the Captivate2019Data folder.

2. Preview the video.

   This video is similar to the other videos you have played with during this module. However, there is a significant amount of time at the beginning of the video where the mouse is just moving around the screen and nothing of substance is being demonstrated. You'll trim out that part of the video next.

3. Trim out the first few seconds of the video.

   ☐ close the preview

   ☐ on the Timeline, ensure the red playhead is located at the far **left** (the beginning of the video)

   ☐ slowly drag the playhead **right** along the Timeline

   As you drag the playhead, you can see the mouse moving around but not really accomplishing anything. The first six seconds of the video need to go.

   ☐ position the playhead on the Timeline at **6** seconds

   ☐ at the bottom of the Timeline, click the **Trim** button

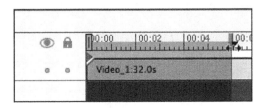

   On the Timeline, **Trim Begin**  and **Trim End** markers appear on either side of the playhead.

   ☐ drag the **Trim Begin** marker all the way to the **left**

   ☐ drag the **Trim End** marker left so that it is lined up with the playhead at **6** seconds

NOTES

☐ at the bottom of the Timeline, click **Trim**

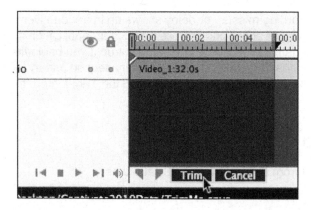

And like magic, the unwanted (selected) portion of the video is gone.

Trimming Confidence Check

1. Ensure that the **TrimMe** video project is still open.

2. The last few seconds of the video need to be trimmed. Go ahead and make it happen.

3. Preview from the beginning of the video to see the newly trimmed video.

4. Save your work and keep the project open.

Assets

Finding quality royalty-free assets for use in your eLearning modules can be a challenge. Keep in mind that if you search the Internet for images, use of any assets you find will likely be governed by a copyright restriction and lead to heavy fines for any unauthorized use. Fortunately, Captivate comes with a wonderful assortment of free assets such as cut out people (pictures of people with the background images and colors removed), icons, 360 assets for virtual reality projects, audio files, and videos. In the activity that follows, you'll insert a Character for use in your Video Demo.

Guided Activity 24: Insert a Character Asset

1. Ensure that the **TrimMe** video project is still open.

2. Ensure that the Playhead is as **far left** on the Timeline as it can go.

3. Insert a Character.

   ☐ choose **Media > Characters**

   The Assets dialog box opens.

   ☐ double-click **any character**
   ☐ from the middle of the dialog box, select **any pose**
   ☐ from the right side of the dialog box, select **Half**

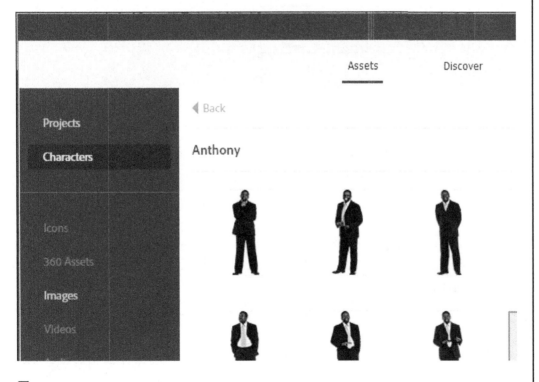

   ☐ click the **Insert** button

Characters Confidence Check

1. Still working in the **TrimMe** project, position the Character similar to the image below.

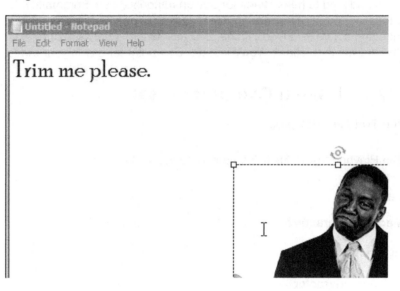

2. Using the **Shapes** tool, draw a Oval Callout on the slide. (You first learned to work with Shapes on page 34.)

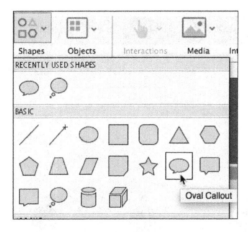

3. Format the callout similar to the image below (double-click the shape to add the text).

4. Preview the beginning of the video to see the new assets that you've added to the project.

5. When finished, save and close the project.

Inserting Video Projects as Slides

It's possible that you'll need to use a Captivate video project in a standard Captivate project. While you cannot import a standard project (cptx) into a video project, it's simple to go the other way around and import video projects (cpvc) into new or existing Captivate projects.

Guided Activity 25: Insert a Video Project

1. Create a new, standard Captivate project.

   ☐ choose **File > New Project > Blank Project**

   The New Blank Project dialog box opens.

   ☐ from the **Select** drop-down menu, choose **800 x 600**

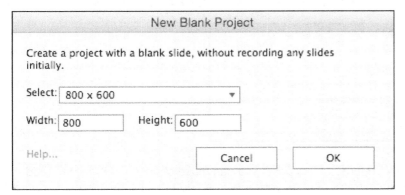

   The size of the existing video project that you'll be importing is already 800 x 600 and it's best to ensure the project sizes are the same.

   ☐ click the **OK** button

2. Insert a video project.

   ☐ choose **Insert > CPVC Slide**

   ☐ from the **Captivate2019Data** folder, open **ImportMe.cpvc**

   The video project is added to the new project and appears on the Filmstrip. Notice that a video slide contains a video icon in the lower right of the Filmstrip thumbnail.

3. Preview the video slide.

   ☐ on the Filmstrip, select slide **2**

   ☐ choose **Preview > From this Slide**

   The video plays beautifully. The ability to insert a video demo into a standard project means that you can combine the ease of creating videos with the interactivity of standard Captivate projects, which is pretty awesome!

4. Close the Preview.

5. Open a video editing session from within a standard project.

   ☐ on the **Filmstrip**, double-click the video slide to open the Properties Inspector

   ☐ on the **Style** tab of the Properties Inspector, click **Edit Video demo**

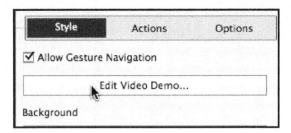

   The video project opens. At this point, you can make changes to the video (add Characters, Video Effects, etc) as you've learned during lessons presented earlier in this module.

   ☐ from the upper left of the Captivate window, click the **Exit** button

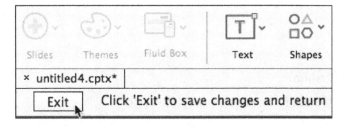

   ☐ click the **Don't save** button

   Because you made no changes to the video project, there are no changes made to the video slide in the untitled Captivate project.

6. Close all projects (there is no need to save).

iCONLOGiC

"Skills and Drills" Learning

Module 5: Captions, Styles, Timing, and Round Tripping

In This Module You Will Learn About:

And You Will Learn To:

Text Captions

Text Captions are typically used to explain a concept being shown onscreen. You can have multiple text captions on the same slide, and you can control how the captions look (to a limited degree), where they appear on the slide, and when they appear (via the Timeline or the Properties Inspector).

Guided Activity 26: Insert and Edit Text Captions

1. Using Adobe Captivate, open the **CaptionMe** project from the **Captivate2019Data** folder.

2. Reset the Classic workspace.

   ☐ choose **Window > Workspace > Reset Classic**

   By resetting the Classic workspace, any inspectors or panels that you might have opened during previous lessons in this book are put away, and your Captivate window should be clutter-free.

3. Preview the lesson.

   ☐ choose **Preview > Project**

   This project is a software simulation that was recorded using Captivate's Demonstration mode (you learned how to create a software demonstration beginning on page 46). The lesson demonstrates the process of creating a new folder on an older version of Windows. While it's a perfectly fine demonstration, there are no Text Captions telling the learner what's about to happen or why. During the next several activities, you will learn how to add Text Captions to several slides. You will also learn how to control the appearance of the captions and when they appear on the slide.

4. Close the Preview.

5. Insert a Text Caption.

   ☐ on the **Filmstrip**, select slide **1**

   ☐ on the toolbar, click **Text** and choose **Text Caption**

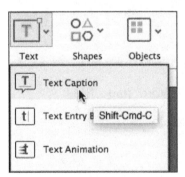

The new Text Caption appears in the middle of the slide.

☐ replace the text in the caption with **Watch as the File menu is selected**

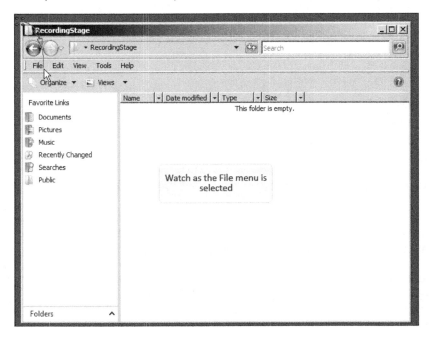

6. Deselect the caption.

☐ click above or below the Text Caption

With the caption deselected, you cannot edit the text within the caption, nor can you change the appearance of the caption or its slide location.

7. Use the Properties Inspector to change the Caption type for a selected Text Caption.

☐ on slide 1, **select the Text Caption**

☐ at the far right of the Captivate window, click **Properties**

Because you selected the text caption on the slide, the Properties Inspector is displaying the properties of the selected caption.

☐ on the **Properties Inspector**, locate the **Caption Type** drop-down menu

☐ from the **Caption Type** drop-down menu, choose **HaloGreen**

8. Resize a Text Caption.

☐ with the Text Caption still selected, position your mouse pointer on one of the Text Caption's resizing handles (the squares)

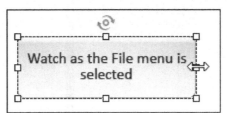

☐ drag the resizing handle until the size of the Text Caption looks good to you

Although the exact size of any Text Caption is always up to you, consider making your Text Captions **narrow** and **tall** as opposed to wide and short. Narrow and tall text captions are typically easier to read than wide and short captions.

Note: As you work with more of the Caption Types, you'll discover that some captions can be made only so small, while other types have fewer limitations on size.

9. Reposition a Text Caption on a slide.

☐ with the Text Caption still selected, drag the middle of the caption toward the **top left** side of the slide and position it so your slide looks similar to the picture below

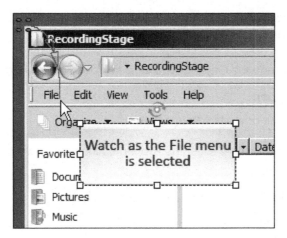

Guided Activity 27: Modify Text Caption Properties

1. Ensure that the **CaptionMe** project is still open.

2. Change the Caption type.

   ❏ on slide **1**, select the Text Caption (if necessary)

   ❏ on the **Properties Inspector**, locate the **Caption Type** drop-down menu

   ❏ from the **Caption Type** drop-down menu, choose **Adobe Red**

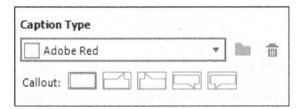

Hey! Did the size of that pesky Text Caption change when you changed the Caption type? There's a very good chance that it did. Why? Captivate's **Autosize Captions** feature is enabled by default. Although the feature might seem like a good thing, I've found that it often forces me to do extra work because Text Captions that I've already resized *magically* resize when I change the way they look (like you just did) or when I edit the text.

3. Disable the Autosize Captions option.

   ❏ Windows users, choose **Edit > Preferences**; Mac users, choose **Adobe Captivate > Preferences**

   ❏ from the top of the Category list at the left, select **Defaults**

   ❏ from the **General** area at the bottom of the dialog box, deselect **Autosize Captions**

   ❏ click the **OK** button

There won't be any visible change to the Text Caption on your slide. You'll see the results of disabling Autosize Captions next.

4. Resize the Text Caption again... this time, make it significantly larger.

5. Use the Properties Inspector to change the Caption Type to **Frosted**.

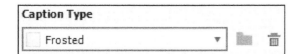

NOTES

NOTES

Although the general appearance of the Text Caption certainly changes, there are no changes to the size of the Text Caption. Is that a good thing or a bad thing? I guess it depends on your perspective. Certainly, if you want Captivate to resize your Text Captions moving forward, turn the Autosize Captions option back on. I always leave the option deselected.

6. Change the character formatting for the caption text.

   ❑ ensure the Text Caption on slide 1 is still selected

   ❑ on the Properties Inspector, locate the **Character** area

   ❑ change the font to **Verdana**

   Note: When selecting Verdana, you won't find it if you scroll too deep down the Font menu. Instead, you'll find it higher in the menu (grouped among the Web Safe fonts). There are two groups of fonts in Captivate: **Web Safe** and **System**. I'd suggest that you always stick with Web Safe fonts. While there are just a few Web Safe fonts from which to choose, most computers (Mac and Windows) have the Web Safe Fonts installed. If you select Web Safe fonts, there's a better chance that you won't run into missing font issues when learners access your eLearning content.

   ❑ change the size to **15 pt**

   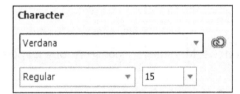

7. Change the appearance of a single word.

   ❑ double-click inside the text caption

   Double-clicking a caption results in the insertion point appearing within the caption. At this point, you can edit the text within the caption and format selected words.

   ❑ double-click the word **File** to highlight it

   ❑ from the **Character** area on the Properties Inspector, select the **Bold** command

   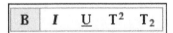

   The Text Caption should look similar to the image below.

   Watch as the **File** menu is selected

Confidence Check

1. Ensure that the CaptionMe project is still open.

2. On slide **1**, change the Caption type for the Text Caption to
   Adobe Blue. (Need help? See page 89.)

3. Go to slide **3**.

4. Insert a Text Caption with the words **Watch as the New command is
   selected**.

   Notice that the formatting of the new Text Caption does not match the appearance of your
   first Text Caption. No worries... you'll learn how to ensure consistent formatting of slide
   objects very soon. For now, you're only concerned with knowing how to insert a Text
   Caption, not necessarily making it look good.

5. Go to slide **4** and insert a new Text Caption that says **Watch as the Folder command is
   selected**.

6. Go to slide **6** and insert a new Text Caption that says **Watch as the new Folder is
   selected**

7. Save and then close the project.

NOTES

Caption Styles

During the activity that began on page 86, you learned how to insert a Text Caption and then how to change its formatting. Did you notice that every time you inserted a Text Caption, the appearance of the caption reverted to a specific Caption type, font, and font size? Although it is easy enough to change the appearance of the caption, you will quickly tire of the effort required to change every caption. Instead, you can alter the way Text Captions appear in this project via Caption Styles. Once you set up the appearance of the Caption Style, all new captions take on the attributes of the style and save you from extensive manual formatting.

Guided Activity 28: Edit the Default Caption Style

1. Using Captivate, open **StyleMe** from the **Captivate2019Data** folder.

2. Go from slide to slide and notice that most of the slides in this project contain a Text Caption. The appearance of each Text Caption is identical (HaloBlue, Calibri, 16 pt).

3. Override a style.

   ☐ go to slide **3** and select the Text Caption

   ☐ using the **Properties Inspector**, change the **Caption Type** to **HaloGreen**

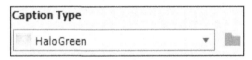

   ☐ from the Character area, change the font to **Verdana** and the size to **15**

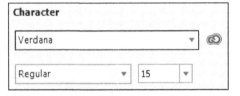

   The three changes you made to the caption have had an obvious effect on the selected Text Caption on slide 3. But what about the Text Captions on the other slides?

4. Explore the other slides.

   ☐ go from slide to slide and notice that none of the other Text Captions have taken on the appearance of the Text Caption on slide 3

5. Observe an Object Style override.

   ☐ return to slide **3** and select the Text Caption that you just formatted

   ☐ at the top of the **Properties Inspector**, locate the **Style Name** area

A style named **[Default Caption Style]** is selected in the drop-down menu, indicating that it's the style being used by the selected Text Caption. In fact, all of the Text Captions in the StyleMe project are using the Default Caption Style, which explains the reason that the appearance of every Text Caption in the project is consistent.

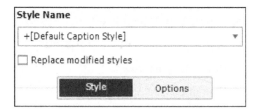

Okay, okay, you caught me. I said above that every Text Caption in the project is using the [Default Caption Style]. I should have stated that *most of the captions are following the [Default Caption Style]*. In fact, the Text Caption on slide 3 is following only a portion of the formatting specified in the style. How can you tell? Take a look at the name of the style in the Style drop-down menu. There's a plus sign to the left of the style's name.

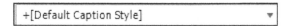

The plus sign indicates that something about the way the caption has been formatted doesn't match the intent of the style. Unfortunately, there's no way to tell exactly what the formatting issue is, but the plus sign is a handy way to quickly determine that the formatting is different in some way.

I'm betting that you don't have a huge staff to support your eLearning development efforts. I'm also pretty sure that you don't have hours to waste on manual labor. If you use the Properties Inspector to format every object on every slide, you'll find yourself formatting and formatting and formatting. And when you're done, you'll format some more. I don't want to even think about how much extra work you will have to deal with if you want (or your boss wants) to update the appearance of the captions throughout the project. For that reason, I discourage you from using the Properties Inspector to change the way any object looks. You'll find it much more efficient to change the way things look via the Object Style Manager (you'll play with that soon). Instead, use the Properties Inspector to change the way objects behave (Timing, Actions, etc.). Those kinds of properties are not controlled by an Object Style.

6. Reset a style.

   ☐ with the Text Caption on slide 3 still selected, click the menu to the right of **Style Name** and choose **Reset Style**

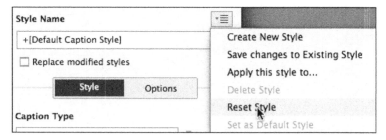

The plus sign goes away, and the selected Text Caption is once again following the properties of the Default Caption Style (HaloBlue, Calibri, 16 pt).

7. Edit the Default Caption Style.

   ☐ choose **Edit > Object Style Manager**

   The Object Style Manager opens.

   ☐ from the top of the Object Style Manager dialog box, select **[Default Caption Style]**

   ☐ from the **Caption** area at the right, change the **Caption Type** to **Frosted**

   ☐ from the **Text Format** area, change the Family to **Verdana**

   ☐ change the Size to **15**

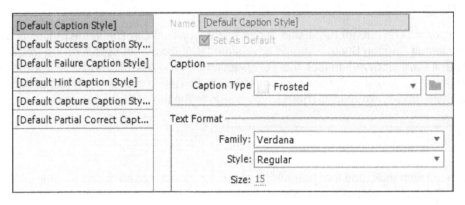

   ☐ click the **OK** button

   Every caption in the project is now using the new Caption type and Text formatting. Don't you love object styles? Make a few edits in one place (the Object Style Manager), and potentially hundreds of slide objects are updated instantly. *Cool!*

8. Save your work.

Callouts

You learned how to apply a Caption type on page 89. While Caption types define the general look of the caption (HaloGreen, Adobe Blue, etc.), Callouts give a Text Caption direction. Most Caption Types include up to five Callouts that point to different areas of the slide. While Caption types are part of an Object Style (page 92), Callouts are options you manually apply to a selected object, one object at a time.

Guided Activity 29: Change a Callout Used by a Text Caption

1. Ensure that the **StyleMe** project is still open.

2. Change the Callout used on a Text Caption.

   ☐ go to slide **1**

   The Callout being used on the Text Caption is a simple rectangle.

   ☐ select the **Text Caption**

   ☐ on the Properties Inspector, select the third Callout

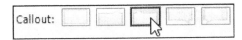

   The caption now points up and to the left. The arrow helps guide the learner's eye toward the area of the screen where the mouse action is occurring.

Confidence Check

1. Move the Text Caption up and to the left a bit until the position is similar to the image below.

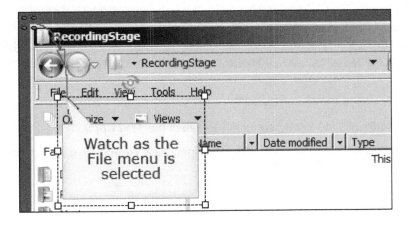

2. Go through the remaining slides and apply the third Callout to the rest of the captions.

3. Position (drag) each of the captions on the slides where you think appropriate.

4. Save and close the project.

The Timeline

The Timeline is at the bottom of the Captivate window. Each slide has a unique Timeline. You can use the Timeline to control the timing of any slide object. For instance, using the Timeline, you can force the captions to appear on the slide at the same time, or you can force one caption to appear as another goes away. The Timeline consists of the following features: Object Bars, a Header, a Playhead, and Playback Controls. The objects on a project slide are displayed as stacked bars on the left side of the Timeline. The Header at the top of the Timeline indicates time in seconds (and parts of seconds). The Playhead shows the point in time in which the slide is being viewed.

Guided Activity 30: Control Slide and Object Timing

1. Using Captivate, open **TimeMe** from the **Captivate2019Data** folder.

2. Display the Timeline.

   ☐ at the bottom of the Captivate window, click **Timeline**

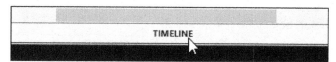

3. Use the Timeline to extend the slide duration to eight seconds.

   ☐ on the Timeline, position your mouse pointer on the far right edge of the **Slide 1** object bar (until your mouse pointer looks like a double-headed arrow)

   ☐ drag the **right edge** of the object to the **right** until you get to **00:08** seconds on the Timeline (the word **End** should line up with the 00:08 mark on the Timeline)

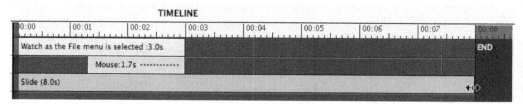

4. Extend slide timing using the slide Properties.

   ☐ click in the middle of slide 1 (be careful not to select the Text Caption)

   ☐ open the **Properties Inspector** and, from the right, click **Timing** to open the **Timing Inspector**

   ☐ change the **Slide Duration** to **10** sec

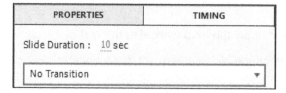

On the Timeline, notice that changing the Display Time on the Properties Inspector is exactly the same thing as dragging the right edge of the slide object to 10 seconds on the Timeline.

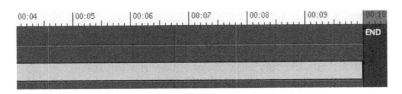

5. Use the Timeline to extend the display time for a Text Caption.

   ☐ on the **Timeline**, select the object **"Watch as the File menu is selected"**

   This object represents the **Watch as the File menu is selected** Text Caption on the slide.

   ☐ on the **Timeline**, drag the **right edge** of the **"Watch as the File menu is selected"** object **right** until the object is stretched to **00:04** seconds

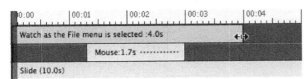

6. Use the Timeline to change the timing for the mouse.

   ☐ still working on slide 1, select the **Mouse** object on the Timeline

   This object represents the mouse pointer on the slide.

   ☐ drag the middle of the **Mouse object** right until its left edge lines up with **00:04** on the Timeline

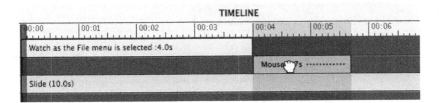

NOTES

Confidence Check

1. Still working in the TimeMe project, change the Slide Duration for slide **1** to **5.7** seconds.
   (Need help? See page 96.)

2. Preview the first five slides.

   The Text Caption on slide **1** should play for four seconds. After the Text Caption disappears from the slide, the mouse pointer should move from the upper left of the slide to the slide's File menu. Once the action on slide **1** finishes, you're off to slide **2**.

   While on slide **2**, notice that it takes too much time for the click to actually occur—the timing needs work.

3. Close the preview and go to slide **2**. On the Timeline, select the **Mouse** object and, using the **Timing Inspector**, change the **Appear After** to **0 sec**.

4. From the **Timing** area, change the **Display For Specific Time** to **0.5 sec**

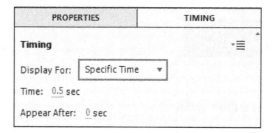

5. On the Timeline, change the Slide Duration to **0.5** sec.

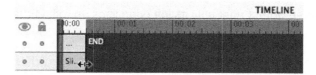

6. Starting with slide **1**, preview the **Next 5 Slides**. When you get to slide **2**, the timing of the mouse click should be better.

7. Change the timing for slides **3**, **4**, and **6** as follows:

   Text Captions: Appear After **0 sec**; Display For Specific Time: **4 sec**

   Mouse objects: Appear After **4 sec**; Display For Specific Time: **1.7 sec**

   Slide Duration: **5.7 sec**

8. Change the timing for slide **5** as follows:

   Mouse object Appears After: **0 sec**; Displays For Specific Time: **0.5 sec**

   Slide Duration: **0.5 sec** (**Note:** If you have trouble using the Properties Inspector to change the Slide Duration to 0.5, use the Timeline.)

9. Preview the project. The timing between slides and objects should be smooth. When finished, close the preview, save, and close the project.

Guided Activity 31: Check Spelling

1. Open **SpellMeAlignMe** from the **Captivate2019Data** folder.

   This is pretty much the same project you've been working on since the beginning of this module. To save you a little work, I've added an introduction slide that explains the upcoming lesson. I timed the Text Captions so that each one plays for five seconds and appears on the slide one after the other.

2. Disable Calculate Caption Timing.

   ☐ Windows users, choose **Edit > Preferences**;
   Mac user, choose **Adobe Captivate > Preferences**

   ☐ from the top of the dialog box, select **Defaults**

   ☐ from the **General** area, deselect **Calculate Caption Timing**

   ☐ Autosize Captions
   ☐ Calculate Caption Timing

   Depending on how you look at the world, the Calculate Caption Timing feature is one of those "glass half empty, half full" kind of commands. With the option selected, Captivate automatically calculates how long a caption stays on a slide based on the number of characters in the caption. *That's a glass half-full kind of thing—you don't have to worry about the timing.*

   However, if you select a specific display time (as you have done with the captions in this project) and then change a caption's content, you would inadvertently reset your specified time to Captivate's calculated caption timing. *That's a glass half-empty kind of thing— you'll have to reset the timing via the Timeline or through the Text Caption's properties.* I always disable Calculate Caption Timing.

   ☐ click the **OK** button

3. On slide **1**, notice that there are typos in the Text Captions (from misspelled words to double words). No worries, you'll be fixing each of the typos during the Check Spelling activity that follows.

4. Spell check the project.

   ☐ choose **Project > Check Spelling**

   The Check Spelling dialog box opens. The first word that is flagged as Not In Dictionary is the word **foolders**. It should be replaced with the word **folders**.

NOTES

❑ ensure that **folders** is selected in the **Suggestions** area

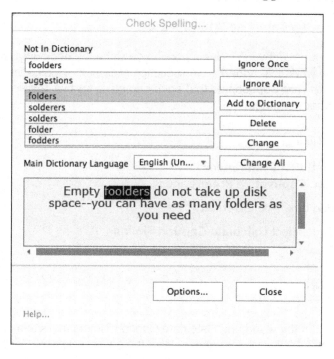

❑ click the **Change** button

The next error is the double word "you."

❑ click the **Delete** button

The word "demmonstration" is flagged as Not In Dictionary.

❑ select **demonstration** from the list of Suggestions and then click the **Change** button

The double word "is" is flagged.

❑ click the **Delete** button

The word "seelected" is flagged as Not In Dictionary.

❑ select **selected** from the list of Suggestions and then click the **Change** button

Once the Spell Check is complete, you are alerted to the total number of corrections made.

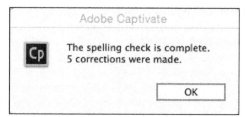

❑ click the **OK** button

Guided Activity 32: Align Slide Objects

1. Ensure that the **SpellMeAlignMe** project is still open.

2. Hide an object.

   ❑ go to slide **1**

   There are four Text Captions on the slide. You'll soon use Captivate's alignment features to line up three of the four captions. One of the captions is in the way. Rather than drag it out of the way, only to have to drag it back, it is more efficient to temporarily hide it.

   ❑ if necessary, display the **Timeline** (you learned how to display the Timeline on page 96)

   ❑ on the left side of the Timeline, click the first circle just beneath the eyeball

   The circle becomes a red x. The "**During this demonstration**" caption disappears from the slide (although it's still visible on the Timeline).

   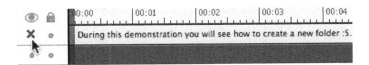

   With the top-most caption hidden, you can easily see the three remaining captions. Even though the caption is hidden from view, it will still preview and publish.

3. Select multiple captions.

   ❑ click one time on the caption containing "New folders can be..."

   ❑ press and hold the [**shift**] key on your keyboard

   ❑ click one time on the caption containing "You can give your folder..."

   ❑ keep the [**shift**] key down on your keyboard

   ❑ click one time on the caption containing "Empty folders do not take..."

   ❑ release the [**shift**] key

   All three captions should be selected.

4. Left-align the selected captions.

   ❑ choose **Modify > Align > Align Left**

   The selected objects aligned to the left.

   ❑ choose **Modify > Align > Distribute Vertically**

   The captions are now lined up with the first caption you selected (objects with white handles serve as anchors, and other selected objects move to the anchors when you align objects). In addition, the vertical space between the selected captions is evenly spaced.

Confidence Check

1. Ensure that the **SpellMeAlignMe** project is still open.

2. Ensure you are on slide **1**, and choose **Preview > Next 5 slides**.

3. As slide **1** plays, notice that the timing of the Text Captions is pretty good. But don't you think it would be better if the three Text Captions (after the first one) stayed around for the duration of the slide? Sure you do!

4. Close the preview and return to slide **1**.

5. Select all three of the visible Text Captions on slide **1** (the first Text Caption should still be hidden).

6. Choose **Modify > Show for the rest of the slide**.

   On the Timeline, notice that the selected objects have stretched to the end of the slide.

7. Preview the first five slides.

   Notice that after the first Text Caption goes away, the remaining captions show for the rest of the slide.

8. Show the hidden Caption.

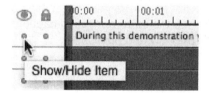

9. Close the preview.

10. Keep the project open for the next activity.

Round Tripping

Exporting captions to Microsoft Word is one of my favorite Captivate features. Why? If you export the captions to Word, any team member can open the exported document with Word and make editorial changes. Those changes can be *imported into Captivate*—something I call **Round Tripping**.

You can use this round trip work-flow to create multiple-language versions of your project without having to rerecord or re-create the project. All you have to do is send the exported captions to a translator and have the caption text translated into another language. You would then import the translated captions back into your project. *Cool!*

Guided Activity 33: Export Captions to Microsoft Word

1. Ensure that the **SpellMeAlignMe** project is still open.

2. Export the project captions.

   ☐ choose **File > Export > Project Captions and Closed Captions**

   The Save As dialog box opens.

   ☐ ensure that you are saving to the **Captivate2019Data** folder as **SpellMeAlignMe Captions**

   ☐ click the **Save** button

   Note: Mac users, you may see a **Grant File Access alert**. If so, click **Select**, open the **Captivate2019Data** folder and click **Grant Access**.

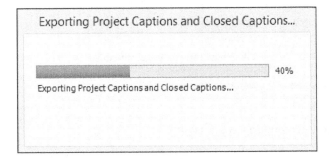

Exporting Project Captions and Closed Captions...

40%

Exporting Project Captions and Closed Captions...

   You are notified when the captions have been exported.

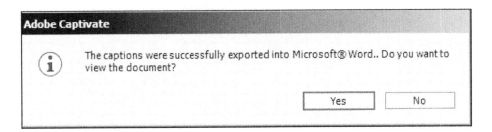

Adobe Captivate

The captions were successfully exported into Microsoft® Word.. Do you want to view the document?

| Yes | No |

   ☐ click the **Yes** button to open the Word document

   The captions have been imported into a Word table. There are five columns with the following headers: **Slide Id**, **Item Id**, **Original Text Caption Data**, **Updated Text Caption Data**, and **Slide**. You can make any changes you want to the Updated Text Caption Data,

NOTES

but you must not change any of the other information. The slide ID identifies to which slide your edited captions go. The Item ID identifies which caption goes with which caption data.

Adobe Captivate			Sunday, August 26, 2018	
Slide Id	Item Id	Original Text Caption Data	Updated Text Caption Data	Slide
2797	2773	Empty folders do not take up disk space--you can have as many folders as you need	Empty folders do not take up disk space--you can have as many folders as you need	1
2797	2777	You can give your folder any name up to 255 characters	You can give your folder any name up to 255 characters	1
2797	2781	New folders can be created in any window	New folders can be created in any window	1
2797	2785	During this demonstration you will see how to create a new folder	During this demonstration you will see how to create a new folder	1
899	2676	Watch as the File menu is selected	Watch as the File menu is selected	2
947	2711	Watch as the New command is selected	Watch as the New command is selected	4
962	2715	Watch as the Folder command is selected	Watch as the Folder command is selected	5
992	2719	Watch as the new Folder is selected	Watch as the new Folder is selected	7

3. Update the Word content.

   ☐ on slide ID **2797**, Item ID **2785**, find the phrase **During this demonstration you will see...** in the **Updated Text Caption Data** column

   ☐ change the text to **During this lesson, you will see... .**

window	window	
During this demonstration you will see how to create a new folder	During this lesson, you will see how to create a new folder	1
Watch as the File menu is selected	Watch as the File menu is selected	2
Watch as the New command is selected	Watch as the New command is selected	4
Watch as the Folder command is selected	Watch as the Folder command is selected	5
Watch as the new Folder is selected	Watch as the new Folder is selected	7

4. Save the Word document and exit/quit Microsoft Word.

5. Return to the Captivate project.

Guided Activity 34: Perform a Round Trip

1. Ensure that the **SpellMeAlignMe** project is still open.

2. Import the edited caption into the Captivate project.

   ☐ choose **File > Import > Project Captions and Closed Captions**

   The Open dialog box appears.

   ☐ open **SpellMeAlignMe Captions** from the **Captivate2019Data** folder

   You will be notified that the items were imported into the project.

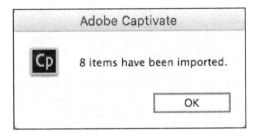

   ☐ click the **OK** button

3. Review the updated caption.

   ☐ go to slide **1**

   Notice that the text you changed in the Word document has been updated on the slide. How awesome is that?

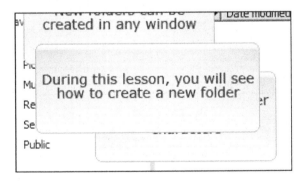

4. Save your work and close the project.

Notes

iCONLOGiC
"Skills and Drills" Learning

Module 6: Pointers, Paths, Boxes, and Buttons

In This Module You Will Learn About:

- Mouse Effects, page 108
- Pointer Paths and Types, page 110
- Highlight Boxes, page 113
- Image Buttons, page 116

And You Will Learn To:

- Control Mouse Effects, page 108
- Edit a Mouse Path, page 110
- Clone an Object Style, page 113
- Insert a Highlight Box, page 114
- Insert an Image Button, page 116
- Control Appear After Timing, page 119

Mouse Effects

If your lesson is intended to demonstrate an application on your computer, including the Mouse pointer is a good idea. If you do include the Mouse pointer, you can control the speed of the mouse, its exact starting and ending slide position, include visual Mouse clicks, and enable a click sound to further enhance the learner experience.

Guided Activity 35: Control Mouse Effects

1. Open **MouseVisualMe** from the **Captivate2019Data** folder.

2. Preview the project.

   ❑ choose **Preview > Project**

   This project is very similar to the one you were working on previously. As the Mouse moves from slide to slide, notice that there is no visual indicator that a click is occurring, and no sound to accompany the click.

3. Add a click sound to the Mouse.

   ❑ close the preview and then go to slide **4**

   This is where the Mouse goes to the **File** menu and the menu is clicked. It's the perfect place to add both a visual Mouse click and click sound.

   ❑ on the **Timeline** double-click the **Mouse** object

   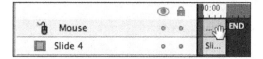

   ❑ on the **Properties Inspector**, select **Mouse Click Sound**

   ❑ ensure **Single-click** is selected from the drop-down menu

   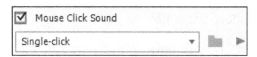

4. Add a visual Mouse click to the Mouse pointer on slide 4.

   ❑ ensure the **Mouse** on slide **4** is still selected

   ❑ on the **Properties Inspector**, select **Show Mouse Click**

   ❑ select **Custom** from the drop-down menu and select any of the Mouse clicks you like from the drop-down menu (you can preview the Mouse click visual by clicking the Play button to the right of the selection)

   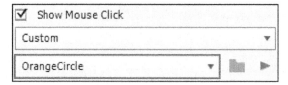

Visual Click Confidence Check

1. Go to slide **3** and preview the next five slides.
   (**Preview > Next 5 slides**)

   When slide **4** plays, you should see and hear the Mouse click.

2. Add a visual Mouse click and Mouse click sound to the Mouse pointer
   on slides **5**, **6**, and **8**.

3. Use the Timing Inspector to change the Transition for slide **2** to **Wipe**.

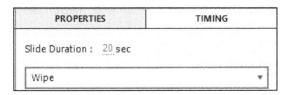

PROPERTIES	TIMING
Slide Duration : 20 sec	
Wipe ▾	

4. Save your work.

5. Preview the project.

   As the lesson plays, pay particular attention to the **Wipe** transition you added that softens
   the abrupt jump between slides 1 and 2. In addition, notice the visual Mouse clicks and
   sounds you added.

6. When the preview is finished, close the preview.

7. Save and close the project.

Pointer Paths and Types

When you record a lesson using Captivate, every move you make with the Mouse can be recorded, including menu selections, dialog box selections, and the path your Mouse takes as you move it around the screen. Captivate includes the ability to easily change the pointer path without having to re-record the lesson.

After you record a Demonstration (you learned how on page 47) that includes the Mouse cursor, you can change the way the Mouse pointer looks on a single Captivate slide or throughout the project. The pointer can be changed to a variety of icons, such as a hand, a vertical resize pointer, or a drag pointer. If you are not happy with the pointer icons that come with Captivate, you can select any system pointer or existing CUR (cursor) file on your hard drive or network as the pointer image.

Guided Activity 36: Edit a Mouse Path

1. Open **PointerPathMe** from the **Captivate2019Data** folder.

2. Hide a slide object.

    ☐ go to slide **3**

    ☐ on the **Timeline,** look to the left of the caption containing the words "Watch as..."

    ☐ click **Show/Hide Item** (the little circle just beneath the eyeball icon)

The little circle turns into a red X when clicked. The Show/Hide Item is a toggle. To Show an item, click the red X, and it returns to the shape of a circle.

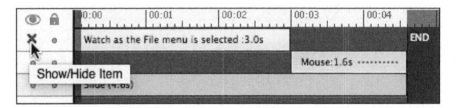

With the selected caption hidden, it's easier to focus on the slide's Mouse pointer. Notice that the tip of the pointer (the tip of the Mouse pointer is often referred to as the "hot spot") is pointing just to the right of the "e" in "File." It might look a bit better if the hot spot of the Mouse pointer is optically centered over the word "File."

3. Edit the pointer path.

   ☐ drag the Mouse pointer **up** and to the **left** just a bit so that it is more optically centered over the word **File**

During the recording process (you learned about recording screen actions on page 46), it's possible that you made a mistake and clicked the wrong part of the screen. In that instance, Captivate creates a screen capture, and your Mouse is shown in the wrong part of the screen. *Ouch!* You've just learned that you can move the Mouse pointer location in Captivate *after the recording process*. How slick is that? Re-record a lesson? I don't think so!

4. Still on slide **3**, **show** the text caption that you hid a moment ago.

5. Go to slide **4**.

   Notice that the Mouse pointer on slide 4 didn't get the memo from the Mouse pointer on slide 3 (informing it that it needs to move up and to the left). You can get a better look at the problem by switching between slides 3 and 4, and you see the pointer jump between the two slides. Hold on for a bit of magic as you tell the pointer on slide 4 to match the position of the pointer on slide 3.

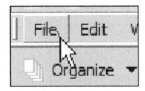

6. Align the slide position of the Mouse pointer with the previous slide.

   ☐ still working on slide **4**, select the Mouse pointer

   ☐ choose **Modify > Mouse > Align to Previous slide**

   The position of the Mouse pointer on slide 4 should now match the position you established for the Mouse pointer on slide 3. Without this wonderful feature, you would have been forced to drag the pointer on slide 4 a bit at a time, and then constantly switch between slides 3 and 4 to ensure that the alignment is perfect. The **Align to** feature makes quick work of the process.

7. Change the Mouse pointer type.

   ☐ go to slide **9**

   Notice the mouse pointer type is a standard white pointer.

   ☐ on the slide, select the Mouse pointer

☐ on the **Properties Inspector**, **Display** area, select the **Hand Pointer** (if you don't see the Hand Pointer, click the **>** to see more options)

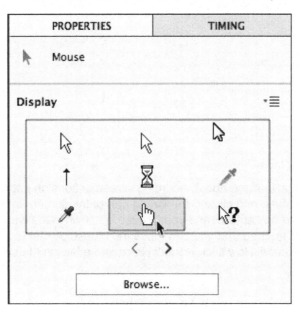

On the slide, the Mouse pointer now looks like a hand pointer. This change affects only the pointer on slide **9**.

Note: If you wanted to use this pointer type on all of the pointers in the current project, you could right-click the pointer on the slide and choose **Use the current mouse pointer for all slides**.

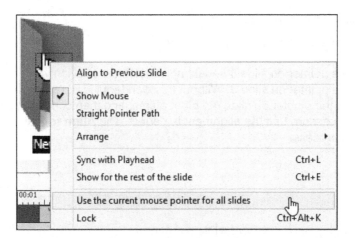

8. Save your work.

Highlight Boxes

Highlight Boxes provide a great way to grab the learner's attention. They are particularly helpful if a slide is cluttered or visually distracting. Like most objects in Captivate, you can control the appearance of Highlight Boxes via Object Styles, and control the length of time they are onscreen via the Timeline or the Timing Inspector.

Guided Activity 37: Clone an Object Style

1. Ensure that the **PointerPathMe** project is still open.

2. Clone an existing style.

   ❒ choose **Edit > Object Style Manager**

   ❒ at the far left of the dialog box, click the triangle to expand the **Standard Objects**

   ❒ select **Highlight Box**

   ❒ from the middle column, select **[Default Blue Highlight Box Style]**

   ❒ at the bottom of the column, click the **Clone** button

   The selected style has been duplicated. You can now give the duplicate any name you like and then edit its attributes.

   ❒ in the Name area at the right, change the name to **Custom Highlight Box Style**

   ❒ from the **Fill & Stroke** area, select any Fill, Stroke Color, and Width you like

   ❒ change the Transition to **Fade In Only**

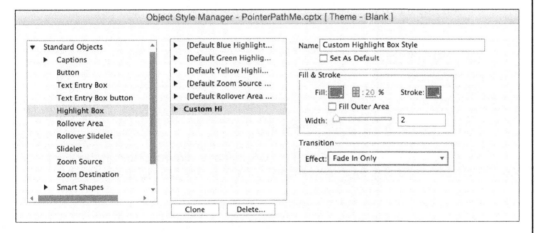

   ❒ click the **OK** button

Guided Activity 38: Insert a Highlight Box

1. Ensure that the **PointerPathMe** project is still open.

2. Insert a Highlight Box.

    ☐ go to slide **3**

    ☐ choose **Objects > Highlight Box**

    The New Highlight Box box appears on the slide using the attributes of the [Default Blue Highlight Box Style].

3. Apply a different style to the new Highlight Box.

    ☐ from the **Style Name** drop-down menu on the **Properties Inspector**, choose **Custom Highlight Box Style**

    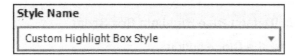

    The appearance of the selected Highlight Box should match the attributes of the style you created a moment ago. If you are unhappy with the appearance of the object, you can at any time return to the Object Style Manager, select the style, and edit it.

4. Resize and reposition the Highlight Box.

    ☐ on the slide, drag the Highlight Box **up** and to the **left** and resize it so that it covers just the **File** menu

5. Review object timing on the Timeline.

    On the Timeline, notice that the Text Caption and Highlight Box are both set to appear right away and play for three seconds. After that, the Mouse appears.

    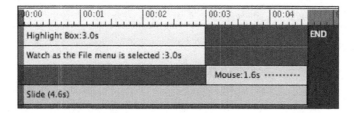

6. Preview a single slide.

    ☐ choose **Preview > Play slide**

    As expected, the Highlight Box fades in as the slide plays and stays around as long as the text caption. Then the Mouse does its thing. However, the timing for the caption is a bit off. You might have noticed that the caption stuck around a tiny bit longer than the Highlight

Box. The reason? The Highlight Box has a Transition of Fade In Only. The caption's Transition is set to Fade In and Out. You'll change that next.

7. Update and then save changes to an existing style.

❑ select the **Text Caption** on slide **3**

❑ on the **Timing Inspector,** change the **Transition** to **Fade In Only**

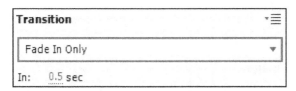

❑ select the **Properties Inspector**

From the Style Name area at the top of the Properties Inspector, notice the plus sign to the left of the Default Caption Style. The plus sign indicates changes have been made to the selected caption that do not match the attributes of the style.

❑ click the menu at the right of **Style Name** and choose **Save changes to Existing Style** button

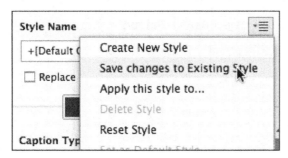

The attributes for all of the captions in the project have been updated and now reflect the Fade In Only Transition.

8. Play the slide.

Now the timing and effects for both the Highlight Box and Text Caption match.

9. Save the project.

Image Buttons

Earlier in this book (page 34) you were introduced to buttons. During the next few activities, you'll take a deeper look at buttons, including controlling timing and adding Image buttons.

Guided Activity 39: Insert an Image Button

1. Ensure that the **PointerPathMe** project is still open.

2. Set Image buttons as the default button style.

   ☐ choose **Edit > Object Style Manager**

   ☐ at the far left of the dialog box, click the triangle to expand the **Standard Objects** area

   ☐ select **Button**

   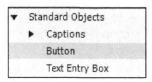

   ☐ from the middle of the dialog box, select **[Default Image Button Style]**

   ☐ from the right side of the dialog box, select **Set As Default**

   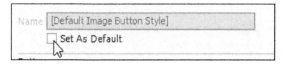

3. Select an image for the image button.

   ☐ from the **Button** area, scroll down and select any image you like (when making your selection, consider that the button will be used by the learner to get to the next slide... the image you choose should reflect the button's intended Action)

   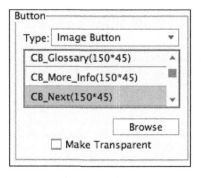

   ☐ click the **OK** button

4. Insert the image button onto a slide.

   ☐ select slide **1**

   ☐ choose **Interactions > Button**

An image button is added to the middle of the slide. Next you'll control what happens when the learner interacts with the button. The **Actions** tab on the **Properties Inspector** has several options in the **On Success** drop-down menu. For instance, you can select **Continue**. With this Action selected, the slide continues to play the remaining time on the Timeline before the learner is taken to the next slide. Alternatively, you can elect to jump the learner to a specific slide in the project. Or you can elect to have the button play a sound. In this instance, you'd like the button to take the learner to the next slide when the button is clicked.

5. Set the button's Action.

   ☐ ensure the **Button** is selected

   ☐ on the **Properties Inspector**, select the **Actions** tab

   ☐ from the **On Success** drop-down menu, ensure **Go to the next slide** is selected

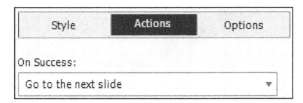

Next you'll set the timing for the button. Although you can do whatever you want with the timing, in this instance, you'd like the button to appear on the slide right away and stick around as long as the slide plays.

6. Set the button's Timing.

   ☐ ensure the button is still selected

   ☐ select the **Timing Inspector**

   ☐ from the **Display For** drop-down menu, select **Rest of Slide**

   ☐ ensure that **Appear After** is set to **0 sec**

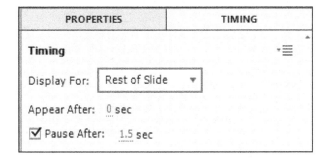

NOTES

7. Resize and reposition the button similar to the picture below.

8. Preview the Next 5 slides.

   As the first slide plays, notice that the action stops too soon—not all of the slide objects have had a chance to appear. You will fix that problem next.

9. Close the preview.

Guided Activity 40: Control Appear After Timing

1. Ensure that the **PointerPathMe** project is still open.

2. Edit a button's Properties so that it pauses the slide after an appropriate amount of time.

   ☐ select the Button on slide **1**

   ☐ select the **Timing Inspector**

   ☐ change **Pause After** to **4.5** seconds

   Setting **Pause After** to 4.5 seconds gives the other slide objects enough time to appear on the slide before the slide action stops.

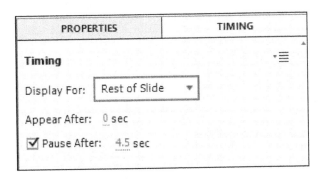

3. Edit the Properties of the button to show a Hand Cursor.

   ☐ select the **Properties Inspector**

   ☐ on the **Actions** tab, **Others** area, select **Hand Cursor**

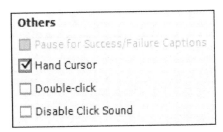

4. Preview the First 5 slides.

   After slide 1 appears, notice that all of the slide elements show up on the slide, and then the lesson stops—waiting for you to click the button.

5. Position your Mouse pointer over the button and notice that your Mouse pointer changes to a hand Mouse cursor—thanks to the **Hand Cursor** option you selected.

6. Click the button to jump to the next slide in the lesson.

7. Close the preview, and then save and close the project.

Notes

iCONLOGiC
"Skills and Drills" Learning

Module 7: Images and Videos

In This Module You Will Learn About:

And You Will Learn To:

Images

Captivate lets you import several graphic formats onto a slide including, but not limited to, native **Photoshop** documents (PSDs), **BMPs** (Windows Bitmap), **GIFs** (Graphics Interchange Format), **JPG** or **JPEG** (Joint Photographic Expert Group), **ICOs** (icons), **WMFs** (MetaFiles), **EMFs** (Enhanced MetaFiles), and **PNGs** (Portable Network Graphics). Once an image has been imported into a project, you can resize it, crop it, and apply multiple effects to it. You'll also find that the image is represented in Captivate's Library. Once in the Library, items can quickly be added to any slide.

Guided Activity 41: Insert, Resize, and Restore an Image

1. Open **Images_Video_Finished** from the **Captivate2019Data** folder.

2. Preview the project.

   The project is loaded with images, audio, and videos. You'll learn how to add the images and videos during this module. You'll learn how to work with audio in the "Audio" module which begins on page 141.

3. Close the preview.

4. Close the project (do not save if prompted).

5. Open **ImageMe_VideoMe** from the **Captivate2019Data** folder.

   This project is nearly identical to the Images_Video_Finished project. Of course, most of the images are missing... and that's where you come in. Let's add some images to this project.

6. Insert an image onto slide 2.

   ☐ go to slide **2**

   ☐ choose **Media > Image**

   ☐ navigate to the **Captivate2019Data** folder and open the **images** folder

   ☐ open **PPE.png**

   The image is inserted in the middle of the slide. Because you will be adding three more images to the slide, it's a good idea to move the current image out of the way.

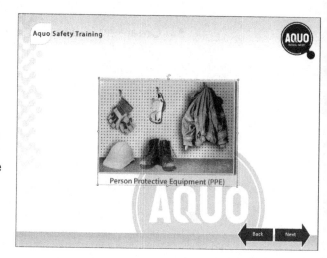

7. Drag the image a few inches to the left on the slide.

8. Insert another image.

   ❑ still working on slide **2**, choose **Media > Image**

   ❑ navigate to the **Captivate2019Data** folder and open the **images** folder

   ❑ open **ShopSafety.png**

9. Position the two images side by side similar to what is shown below.

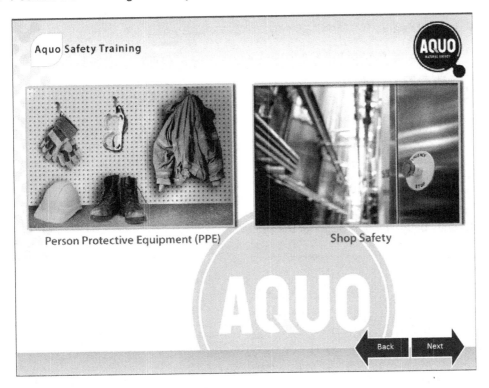

10. Save your work.

NOTES

The Library

Your slides can contain audio, background images, images, animations, linked PowerPoint presentations, and more. Those assets are monitored by Captivate's Library. From the Library, you can add previously imported assets onto any slide by dragging the object's name onto the slide.

Guided Activity 42: Import Images into the Library

1. Ensure that the **ImageMe_VideoMe** project is still open.

2. Show the Library.

   ☐ from the top right of the Captivate window, click **Library**

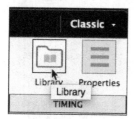

   The Library opens in place of the Properties Inspector. The assets listed in the Library are currently being used throughout the project.

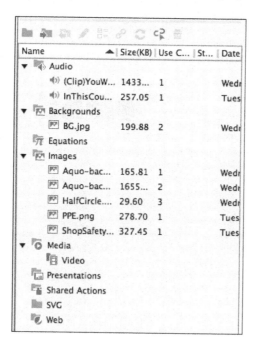

3. Import images into the Library.

   ☐ from just below the Preview area on the Library, click **Import**

☐ navigate to the **Captivate2019Data** folder and open the **images** folder

☐ select **Preventivesafety.png**

☐ PC users; press [**ctrl**] and select **WarehouseSafety**;
   Mac users; press [**cmd**] and select **WarehouseSafety**

Both of the image files should now be selected.

☐ click the **Open** button

☐ click the **OK** button to acknowledge the successful import

Adobe Captivate - ImagesMe_VideoMe.cptx

Cp   2 items have been successfully imported.

OK

The newly imported images are listed in the Library but are not currently being used in the project. (You can confirm the image usage via the Use Count column. Notice that the two newly-imported images have a zero to the right of each image name.)

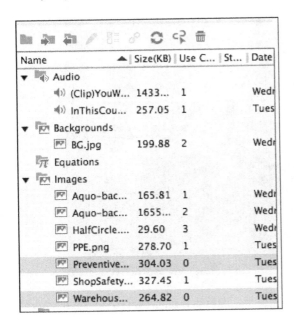

4. Add a Library asset to a slide.

   ☐ on the **Library**, drag **WarehouseSafety** onto slide **2**

5. Move the image a bit to the left to make room for a fourth and final image.

6. Add another Library asset to a slide.

   ☐ on the **Library**, drag **PreventiveSafety** onto slide **2**

With the four images added to the slide, the slide is a bit crowded. In the next activity, you'll learn how to resize and align images.

7. Save your work.

Guided Activity 43: Resize, Transform, and Align Images

1. Ensure that the **ImageMe_VideoMe** project is still open.

2. Manually resize an image.

   ☐ still working on slide **2**, select the **Warehouse Safety** image

   ☐ position your mouse over the **resizing handle** (the white square) in the lower right of the image

   ☐ drag the resizing handle diagonally **up** and to the **left** to make the image much **smaller**

Although resizing an image by dragging its handles is perfectly fine in some instances, you could easily end up with a resized image that is out of proportion (either too tall or too wide). You'll learn a better way to resize in just a minute. First, let's get the image back to its original size.

3. Reset an image size.

   ☐ with the image is still selected, select the **Style** tab on the **Properties Inspector**

   ☐ click the **Reset To Original Size** button

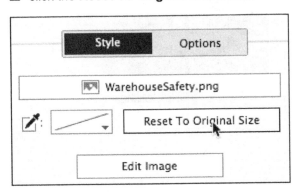

NOTES

The image should be the back to its original size. I often receive questions as to the value of the Reset To Original Size button. Many people believe that it would be just as easy to Undo the image resize as an alternative to clicking the Reset To Original Size button. It's true that clicking the Reset button and using the Undo command achieves the same result. However, the Undo command is valuable only as long as the project is open. If you close the project and save your changes, the Undo command won't work when you reopen the project. The Reset To Original Size button always works.

4. Use the Properties Inspector to change the size of an image.

   ☐ with the **Warehouse Safety** image on slide **2** still selected, click the **Options** tab on the Properties Inspector

   ☐ in the **Transform** area, ensure that **Constrain proportions** is selected

You are about to make the image a bit smaller by changing the W value. With Constrain proportions selected, the height of the image changes proportionally when you change the width.

   ☐ change the **W** value to **343**

The H value should automatically change to **256**.

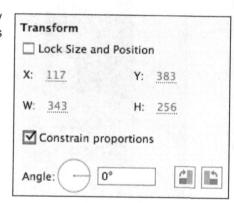

5. Specify a specific slide position for the image.

   ☐ on the **Transform** area, change the **X** value to **117**

   ☐ change the **Y** value to **383**

The X value controls the horizontal position of the selected object; the Y value controls the vertical slide position.

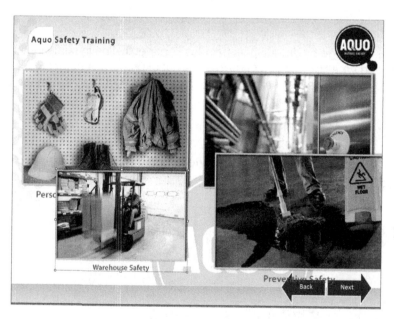

Images Confidence Check

You've resized one of the slide's images, but the other three are still too large. Certainly you could select each image in turn and change its size. But check out this efficient little trick:

1. With the resized and repositioned **Warehouse Safety** image on slide **2** still selected, press [shift] on your keyboard and select each of the remaining three images.

   Note: The selection order is critical. The Warehouse Safety image was already selected. As you selected each of the remaining images, the color of their selection handles is different than those found on the Warehouse Safety image. (Notice that the warehouse image has lighter resizing handles than the other selected images.) The lighter resizing handles visually indicate to you that the selected image is the anchor. As you alter the size of the other images, the anchor will neither resize nor change slide position.

2. Right-click any of the selected images and choose **Align > Resize to the same size**.

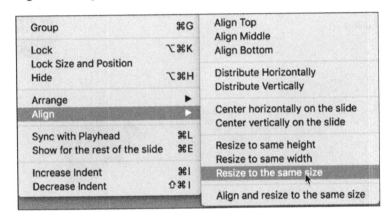

   All four of the selected images are the same size as the Warehouse Safety image.

3. Reposition the images similar to what is shown below. (Experiment with the other alignment options you'll see via right-click, Align.)

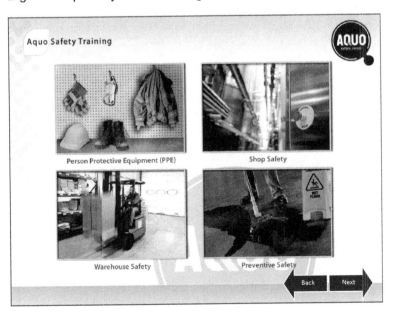

NOTES

4. Import the following images into the Library. (You learned how to do this on page 124.)

☐ boots.png

☐ gloves.png

☐ goggles.png

☐ hat.png

☐ PPE_Group.png

☐ shirt.png

5. Drag the **PPE_Group.png** onto slide **3**

6. Change the width of the **PPE_Group.png** image to **671** (its height should automatically become **469**).

7. Position the **PPE_Group.png** in the middle of the slide.

8. Add the **gloves** image to slide **4** (positioned similar to what is shown below).

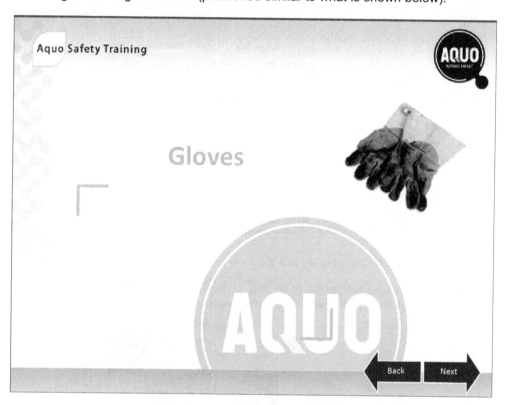

9. Add the **shirt** image to slide **5**, positioned similarly to what you did on slide **4**.

10. Add the **hard hat** image to slide **6**.

11. Add the **boots** image to slide **7**.

12. Add the **goggles** image to slide **8**.

13. Save your work.

Guided Activity 44: Manage Unused Library Assets

1. Ensure that the **ImageMe_VideoMe** project is still open.

2. Insert and delete two images.

   ☐ go to the last slide in the project

   ☐ choose **Media > Image**

   ☐ from the **images** folder, open **betty_baby.jpg**

   ☐ move the image a bit to the left or right of the slide

   ☐ choose **Media > Image**

   ☐ from the **images** folder, open **biff_baby.jpg**

3. Delete both of the images that you just inserted onto the slide. (Click **OK** to acknowledge the deletions.)

   In the Library, notice that the images you deleted are still listed even though they are no longer used in the project. Although unused assets have no effect on the size of a published lesson, unused assets can bloat working project files. I suggest that you routinely remove unused assets from your project (which lowers the overall size of the project file).

NOTES

4. Delete unused Library items.

☐ from the top of the Library, click the **Select Unused Items** tool

Two Library objects are unused. They are now selected and can be deleted.

☐ from the top of the Library, click the **Delete** tool 🗑

☐ click **Yes** to confirm the deletion

5. Save your work.

6. Keep the **ImageMe_VideoMe** project open.

Videos

You can add several types of videos into a Captivate project, including MP4, AVI, MOV, and Flash Video (FLV or F4V). When importing the video, you can elect to import a file directly from your computer or from a web server, Flash Video Streaming Service, or Flash Media Server.

Guided Activity 45: Insert a Video

1. Ensure that the **ImageMe_VideoMe** project is still open.

2. Insert a blank slide.

   ❑ go to slide **1** and choose **Insert > New Slide from > Blank Black Slide**

   The new slide is added after slide 1.

   ❑ on the **Filmstrip**, drag the black slide (slide **2**) above slide **1**

3. Insert a video.

   ❑ with slide **1** selected, choose **Media > Video**

   The Insert Video dialog box opens. You have two choices: Event Video (typically video that is expected to play on only one slide) and Slide Video (video that can play across multiple slides or appear on the TOC). Because the video you'll be working with is expected to play on only the first slide, you'll use Event Video.

   ❑ select **Event Video**

   ❑ from the **Where is your video file?** area, ensure that **On your Computer** is selected and then click the **Browse** button at the right

   ❑ navigate to **Captivate2019Data > videos_animations**

   ❑ open **welcomeToLesson.mp4**

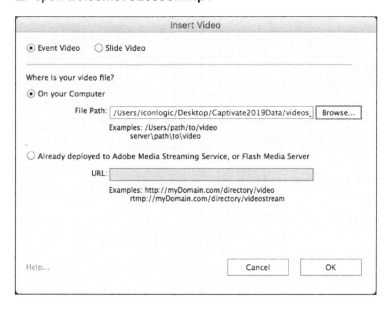

   ❑ click the **OK** button

   The video is imported to the middle of the slide. You will resize the video next.

Guided Activity 46: Set Video Properties

1. Ensure that the **ImageMe_VideoMe** project is still open.

2. Remove the video's skin.

   ☐ with the video on slide **1** selected, go to the **Properties Inspector** and select the **Style** tab

   ☐ from the **Skin** drop-down menu, choose **None**

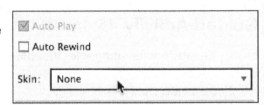

The Skin is a collection of playback controls that overlays a video. Using these controls, learners can pause or mute the video. In this case, you want the video to play without learner interaction. On the **Properties Inspector**, notice that changing the **Skin** to **None** has also made **Auto Play** inactive so the video will play automatically when the lesson is viewed.

3. Change the size of the video.

   ☐ with the video still selected, go to the **Properties Inspector**, **Options** tab

   ☐ from the **Transform** area, ensure **Constrain proportions** is selected

   ☐ change the **W** to **963** and press [**enter**]

Thanks to Constrain proportions, the Height of the video automatically changes to **722**.

4. Change the slide location of the video.

   ☐ with the video still selected and still working on the **Transform** area, change the **X** to **0** and the **Y** to **0**

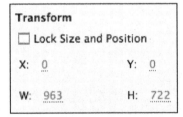

The video should now be completely covering the slide.

5. Set the video timing.

   ☐ with the video still selected, go to the **Timing Inspector**

   ☐ ensure that **Display For** is set to **Rest of Slide**

   ☐ from the **Appear After** area, change the time to **0** sec (so the video plays right away)

   ☐ ensure that **Pause slide till end of video** is selected

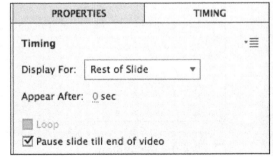

The **Pause slide till end of video** option ensures that the slide sticks around long enough for the video to play.

6. Preview the Next 5 slides.

   A video guide walks onto the stage from the right, introduces the lesson, and then walks off of the stage. How awesome is that?

7. Close the Preview.

8. Add a video to slide 5.

   ☐ go to slide **5** (the Gloves slide)

   ☐ choose **Media > Video**

   ☐ select **Event Video**

   ☐ from the **Where is your video file?** area, ensure that **On your Computer** is selected and then click the **Browse** button

   ☐ navigate to **Captivate2019Data > videos_animations**

   ☐ open **gloves.mp4**

   ☐ click the **OK** button

9. Position and resize the video so that it fits between the green placeholders on the slide.

10. Confirm the video's Timing.

  ☐ on the **Timing Inspector,** ensure that **Display For** is set to **Rest of Slide**

  ☐ from the **Appear After** area, change the time to **0** sec (so the video plays right away)

  ☐ ensure that **Pause slide till end of video** is selected

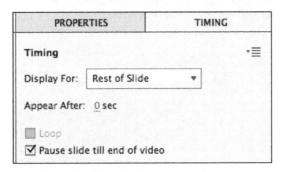

11. Force the video to play automatically.

  ☐ go to the **Properties Inspector, Style** tab

  ☐ select **Auto Play** (put a check in the box)

12. Change the video's skin.

  ☐ from the Skin drop-down menu, choose **clearSkin1**

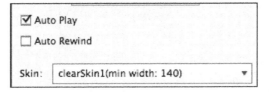

13. Preview the Next 5 slides.

  A video showing a worker putting on the gloves should automatically play.

14. Close the Preview.

15. Save your work.

Videos Confidence Check

1. Import the following videos into the Library. (You first learned how to do this on page 124.)

   ☐ boots.f4v

   ☐ goggles.f4v

   ☐ hardhat.f4v

   ☐ Shirt.f4v

2. Add the appropriate videos to their corresponding slides as **Event** video.

3. Resize each video to fit within the green placeholders.

4. Ensure the **Timing** of each video is such that the video appears right away and displays for the rest of the slide.

5. Ensure each video **Auto Plays**.

6. Ensure that each video uses **clearSkin1**.

7. Go to slide 2 and import the **Safety_Intro** video as **Event** video.

8. Ensure the **Timing** of the video is such that the video appears right away and displays for the rest of the slide.

9. On the **Timing** inspector, deselect **Pause slide till end of video**.

10. Remove the Skin from the video (set the Skin to None).

11. Resize and position the video similar to the image below.

12. Go to the last slide and import the **Safety_Outro** video as **Event** video.

13. Ensure the Timing of the video is such that the video appears right away and displays for the rest of the slide.

14. Remove the Skin from the video.

NOTES

15. Resize and position the video similar to the image below.

16. Preview the project and enjoy all of the videos you've added to the project.

17. Save and close the project.

Image Slideshows

If you have a collection of images on your hard drive or server, you can use Captivate's Image slideshow feature to quickly create a nifty slideshow.

Guided Activity 47: Create an Image Slideshow

1. Create an Image slideshow project.

   ❏ choose **File > New Project > Image Slideshow**

   The New Image Slideshow dialog box appears.

   ❏ from the **Select** drop-down menu, select **640 x 480**

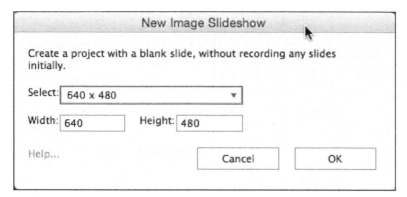

   ❏ click the **OK** button

2. Find the images to be used in the slideshow.

   ❏ from the **Captivate2019Data > images** folder, open the **SlideShowPictures** folder

   There are 15 images within the folder. You will be using all of the images in the Slideshow.

   ❏ select **all** of the images in the folder and then click the **Open** button

   The Resize/Crop Image dialog box opens.

   ❏ click the **OK** button

   The images are imported into a new untitled project and set as the background on each slide.

3. Keep the project open for the Confidence Check that follows.

↑ NOTES ↑

Transitions Confidence Check

1. Preview the project.

   The slideshow works, but the slides move along just a bit too quickly.

2. Close the preview.

3. On the Filmstrip, select the first slide.

4. Scroll down the Filmstrip until you see the last slide.

5. Press [**shift**] and select the last slide. (All of the slides should now be selected, and you can release the [**shift**] key.)

6. On the Timing Inspector, change the **Slide Duration** for the slides to **5** seconds.

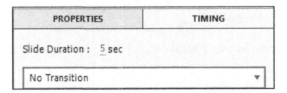

7. Preview the project.

   The timing is better. But wouldn't it be even better to have a transition between one slide and the next? You bet...

8. Select the first slide on the Filmstrip.

9. From the **Transition** drop-down menu on the **Timing Inspector**, select any **Transition** you like.

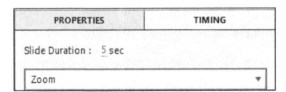

10. Repeat this process for a few more of the slides.

11. When finished, preview the project.

12. Once satisfied with the transitions, close the project. (You can save the project to the **Captivate2019Data** folder with any name that you like, or you can close the project without saving it.)

iCONLOGiC

"Skills and Drills" Learning

Module 8: Audio

In This Module You Will Learn About:

And You Will Learn To:

Rollover Captions

You learned how to create Text Captions earlier in this book. Although similar to Text Captions, Rollover Captions consist of two things: a caption and a rectangular "hot spot" known as the Rollover Area. Rollover Captions appear in your published projects only when the learner moves the mouse over the Rollover Area. Rollover Captions are especially useful for creating tooltips within an application. To see an example of a working tooltip, point to any tool on any Captivate toolbar (the text that appears is a tooltip).

> **Note:** While Rollover Captions (and their close cousins Rollover Images) are certainly cool, rollovers do not work as expected on mobile devices. Because most mobile devices require the user to touch the display to interact with the device, learners need to tap rollover hotspots for the rollover text or image to appear (versus hovering above the hotspots like someone using a mouse would be able to do). Later in this book you will publish your eLearning project as both SWF and HTML5. When publishing as HTML5 there is a utility known as the **HTML5 Tracker**. The Tracker flags anything in your project that would not work as designed on a mobile device. Rollovers are examples of assets that you should not include in your projects if you plan to support mobile learners and/or publish as HTML5.

Guided Activity 48: Insert a Rollover Caption

1. Open **AudioMe** from the **Captivate2019Data** folder.

2. Preview the project.

   This project has similar elements, such as graphics, buttons, and object timing that you have learned about during previous lessons. However, if you hover above the images on slide 2 you'll see Rollover Captions. You'll add a Rollover Caption yourself so you get a feel for how they work.

3. Close the preview.

4. Insert a Rollover Caption onto a slide.

   ☐ go to slide **2**

   ☐ choose **Objects > Rollover Caption**

   Two things appear on your slide: a Rollover Caption and a Rollover Area.

   ☐ type **Excellent, you hit number 1!** into the Text Caption

5. Change the caption's Callout.

   ☐ with just the **Rollover Caption** selected, go to the **Properties Inspector**, **Style** tab

   ☐ select the first **Callout**

6. Move and resize the Rollover Caption.

   ❏ drag the **Rollover Caption** just **above** and to the **right** of the image of the number **1**

   ❏ resize the **Rollover Caption** to suit your taste

7. Move and resize the Rollover Area.

   ❏ drag the **Rollover Area** over the image of the number **1**

   ❏ resize the Rollover Area so that it just covers the image of number **1**

The position of the Rollover Caption and Rollover Area should look similar to the picture below.

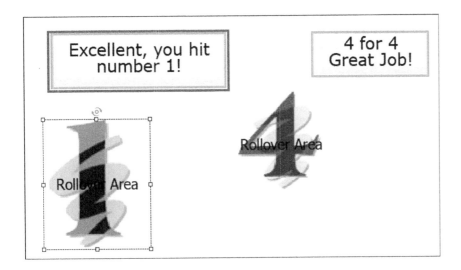

8. Change the Appear After timing for the Rollover.

   ❏ with the **Rollover area** selected, go to the **Timing Inspector** and change the **Appear After** time to **3 sec**.

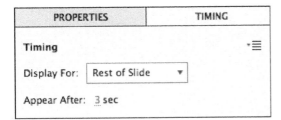

On the Timeline, notice that the left edge of the Rollover Area now lines up with **00:03**. Why did I ask you to make the timing change? Take a further look at the Timeline. The four slide images appear on the slide at the 3-second mark. By delaying the availability of the Rollover Area, you have ensured that overanxious learners won't be able to use the Rollover Area and see the Rollover Caption until the images have appeared on the slide.

9. Preview the project.

10. After the numbers appear on slide 2, point to the number 1.

    Your Rollover Caption should appear and disappear as you move your mouse over and then away from the number 1.

11. Close the preview.

Object Audio

You can import two types of audio files into a Captivate project: WAV and MP3. You can add audio to just about anything. During the activity that follows, you will import audio to some rollover captions and rollover images.

WAV (WAVE): WAV files are one of the original digital audio standards. Although high in quality, WAV files can be very large. In fact, typical WAV audio files can easily take up to *several megabytes of storage per minute* of playing time. If your learner has a slow Internet connection, the download time for large files is unacceptable.

MP3 (MPEG Audio Layer III): Developed in Germany by the Fraunhofer Institute, MP3 files are compressed digital audio files. File sizes in this format are typically 90 percent smaller than WAV files.

> **Note:** To learn more about digital audio formats, visit **www.webopedia.com/ DidYouKnow/Computer_Science/2005/digital_audio_formats.asp**.

Guided Activity 49: Import Audio onto a Slide Object

1. Ensure that the **AudioMe** project is open.

2. Add a sound effect to a Rollover Caption.

   ❑ go to slide **2** and select the **Excellent, you hit number 1!** caption

   ❑ choose **Audio > Import to > Object**

   The Import Audio dialog box opens. By default, you should be taken to the **Sound** folder that comes with Captivate. (If not, navigate to the folder where Captivate is installed (typically Program Files/Adobe/Adobe Captivate 2019/Gallery/Sound on Windows; Go > Applications/Adobe Captivate 2019/Gallery/Sound on a Macintosh.)

   ❑ open **Electronic Tink.mp3**

   The Object Audio dialog box opens.

3. Preview the sound.

   ❑ on the **Add/Replace** tab, click the **Play** button to hear the audio clip

   ❑ click the **Close** button

   The audio file is attached to the selected caption. At this point there is no way to know that the audio file has been attached to the object without previewing. You'll learn later that there is a dialog box called **Advanced Audio Management** that lets you see all of the audio files used in the project (and delete, export, update, and preview them).

Object Audio Confidence Check

1. Preview the project.

2. When you get to slide **2**, use your mouse to point to Image 1.

   The sound effect should play when the Rollover Caption appears.

3. Close the Preview.

4. Attach sounds to the remaining Rollover Captions on slide **2**.

   Note: You can use any of the sound files available in the **Sound** folder or the sound files in the **Captivate2019Data > audio** folder. You will also find hundreds of free sound clips online at **http://www.grsites.com/sounds**.

5. Attach sounds to the Rollover Images on slide **3**.

6. Preview the project. There should be a sound effect attached to each Rollover Caption on slide **2** and to every Rollover Image on slide **3**.

7. When finished, close the preview.

Guided Activity 50: Import Background Audio

1. Ensure that the **AudioMe** project is still open.

2. Import an audio file that plays for the entire project.

   ❑ choose **Audio > Import to > Background**

   ❑ from the **Captivate2019Data > audio** folder, open **2Step1.mp3**

   The Background Audio dialog box opens.

   ❑ from the **Options** area in the lower left of the **Add/Replace** tab, ensure that **Loop Audio** is selected

   The audio file you imported is large enough to play for just over one minute. By selecting Loop Audio, the music plays over and over. Using this technique, you can use shorter audio files for your background music.

   ❑ ensure that **Stop audio at end of project** is selected

   This option ensures that the background music stops when the project is closed by the learner.

   ❑ ensure that **Adjust background audio volume on slides with audio** is selected

   You'll soon be adding voice-over audio to slides 2 and 3. With **Adjust background audio volume on slides with audio** selected, the background music automatically lowers so that you'll be able to hear the voice-over audio without being distracted by the background audio.

   ❑ drag the slider at the right to **15%**

Options:
Fade In: 0 secs   Fade Out: 0 secs
☑ Loop Audio ☑ Stop audio at end of project
☑ Adjust background audio volume on slides with audio: ⊏○━━━━ 15 %

   When adjusting the background audio on slides with audio, the slider controls how much the background audio volume lowers. I've found that 15 percent works reasonably well in most circumstances.

   ❑ click the **Save** button and then click the **Close** button

3. Preview the project.

   You should be able to hear the background music, and when you get to the slides with the sound effects attached to objects, you should still be able to hear the sound effects along with the background audio. Because there isn't any voice-over audio on the slide yet, the volume of the background audio should not yet lower.

4. Close the preview, save, and close the project.

NOTES

Slide Notes

Slide Notes can serve multiple functions. For instance, if you are working with a team of Captivate developers and sharing the Captivate projects, you can add Slide Notes that serve as production comments. If you elect to publish your project as a Word document (handouts), the Notes can be included and appear within the Word document. And because Slide Notes can be displayed when you record voice-overs in Captivate, you can use the Slide Notes as a digital narration script. During the next activity, you will use the Slide Notes feature to add a narration script that you will use when recording your voice (something you will do soon).

Guided Activity 51: Add a Slide Note

1. Open **NarrateMe** from the **Captivate2019Data** folder.

2. Open the Slide Notes panel.

   ☐ go to slide **2**

   ☐ choose **Window > Slide Notes**

   At the bottom of the Captivate window, there is now a **Slide Notes** panel where you can add Closed Captions, convert Text-to-Speech, and add Notes.

   ☐ at the far right of the Slide Notes panel, ensure **Notes** is selected from the **Filter** drop-down menu

3. Add a slide Note.

   ☐ on the Notes panel, click in the space below the triangle at the left and type **Learning to use your mouse is a fundamental computer skill. Practice those skills now by pointing to the numbers that have appeared on this screen.**

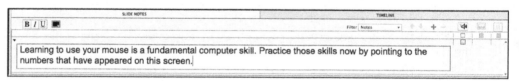

   You will soon use the slide note as a script when you record voice-over audio.

Recording Audio

Captivate allows you to record and edit your own audio. There are three ways to work with sound files: you can attach audio to an entire lesson (running in the background), to an individual slide, or to any object on the slide. If you plan to record your own audio, you first need a microphone connected to your computer. Once you've got the microphone, consider the following:

Setup: If you plan to use high-end audio hardware, such as a mixer or preamplifier, plug your microphone into the hardware and then plug the hardware into your computer's "line in" port. Set the volume on your mixer or preamplifier to just under zero (this will minimize distortion).

Microphone placement: The microphone should be positioned four to six inches from your mouth to reduce the chance that nearby sounds are recorded. Ideally, you should position the microphone above your nose and point it down at your mouth. Also, if you position the microphone just to the side of your mouth, you can soften the sound of the letters *S* and *P*.

Microphone technique: It's a good idea to keep a glass of water close by and, just before recording, take a drink. To eliminate the annoying breathing and lip smack sounds, turn away from the microphone, take a deep breath, exhale, take another deep breath, open your mouth, turn back toward the microphone, and start speaking. Speak slowly. When recording for the first time, many people race through the content. Take your time.

Guided Activity 52: Calibrate a Microphone

1. Ensure that the **NarrateMe** project is still open.

2. Select an Audio Input Device and Bitrate.

   ❑ still working on slide **2**, choose **Audio > Record to > Slide**

   The Slide Audio dialog box opens.

   ❑ at the top of the dialog box, click the link just below the word **Device**

   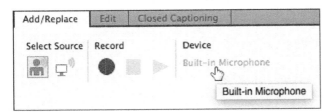

   The Audio Settings dialog box opens.

   ❑ from the **Audio Input Devices, Select** drop-down menu, select your computer's microphone (if you're not sure which device to select, try the one that says Built-In Microphone first)

   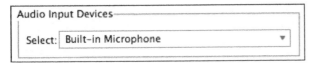

   Note: If there are multiple microphones available in the Select drop-down menu, you'll be playing a game of trial and error. Make your best guess as to which selection to make. If you are unable to calibrate your microphone in the next few moments, return to this drop-down menu and try another microphone.

NOTES

☐ from the Bitrate drop-down menu, ensure that **Constant Bitrate** is selected

Bitrate | Constant Bitrate ▼

Constant Bitrates lead to smaller, nice-sounding audio files. By contrast, Variable Bitrates tend to produce audio with a higher, consistent quality level, but the file sizes are larger than CBRs.

☐ if necessary, change the **Encoding Bitrate** to **FM Bitrate (64kbps)**

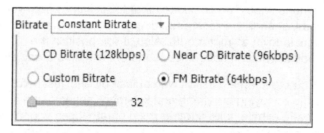

Using a higher Encoding Bitrate setting results in larger published lessons. If you decide to use a higher-quality bitrate than FM Bitrate, you should spend time experimenting with these options to see which selection sounds best. As a general rule, the FM Bitrate is more than adequate for audio that is played through typical computer speakers or headsets.

3. Calibrate the microphone.

    ☐ click the **Calibrate Input** button

    The **Calibrate audio input** dialog box opens. This is where you can set your microphone to its optimum recording level and sensitivity.

    ☐ click the **Auto calibrate** button

    Auto calibrate

    ☐ speaking slowly and clearly, say

    I am setting my microphone recording level for use with Adobe Captivate. While calibrating, it is important that I speak as normally as possible. What I do not want to do is talk either too loudly or too softly.

When the words **Input Level OK** appear beneath the meter at the right, you can stop speaking.

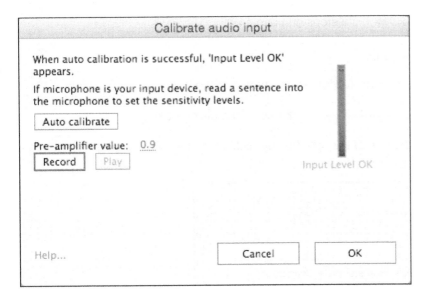

Note: The Pre-amplifier value that you see in the image above is likely not the same value that you get after the Auto calibration process is complete. The Pre-amplifier value varies widely from microphone manufacturer to microphone manufacturer. Generally speaking, the more sensitive your microphone, the lower the Pre-amplifier value will be; the weaker your microphone, the higher the value will be. If the audio that you record audio is faint, try experimenting with the Pre-amplifier value to achieve the ideal results for your setup.

❑ click each of the two **OK** buttons (one to close the Calibrate audio input dialog box and the other to close the Audio settings dialog box)

You should be back at the Slide Audio dialog box, ready to record your audio.

Guided Activity 53: Record Slide Audio

1. Ensure that the **NarrateMe** project is still open. You should have also calibrated your microphone following the steps on page 149.

2. Practice the recording.

   ❏ click the **Captions & Slide Notes** button at the bottom of the dialog box

   The Note you created on page 148 opens in a dialog box.

   ❏ increase the size of the note text by clicking the increase size button (the larger of the two A's)

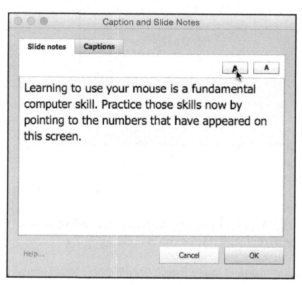

   ❏ take a deep breath and, using a not-too-fast cadence, read the slide Note out loud for practice:

   Learning to use your mouse is a fundamental computer skill. Practice those skills now by pointing to the numbers that have appeared on this screen.

3. Record a narration.

   ❏ from the **Select Source** area of the **Add/Replace** tab, ensure that Narration is selected

   Note: There is also a **System Audio** option in the **Select Source** area. When you select this option, Captivate records the sounds your computer makes while you record. This is especially helpful if you are recording a process on your computer that results in an alert tone. Using System audio, both your narration and the alert tone are recorded.

❑ click the **Record** button in the upper left of the slide Audio dialog box

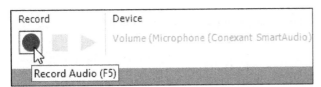

❑ after the countdown goes away, take your time and read the slide Note again: **Learning to use your mouse is a fundamental computer skill. Practice those skills now by pointing to the numbers that have appeared on this screen.**

❑ when finished, click the **Stop** button (located just to the right of the Record button)

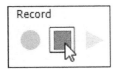

❑ click the **OK** button to close the Caption and Slide Notes dialog box

Your recorded audio appears as a waveform.

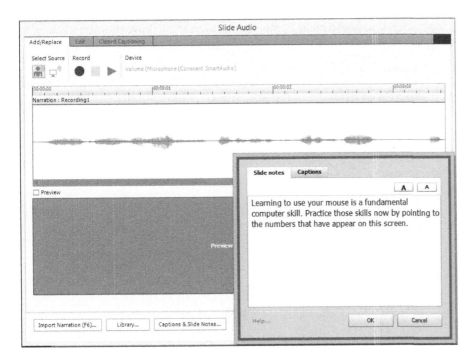

4. Preview the audio.

❑ click the **Play Audio** button, located to the right of the Stop button

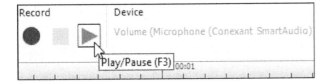

Recording Audio Confidence Check

1. If you are happy with the narration, click the **Save** button in the lower right of the dialog box and then click the **Close** button.

   If you are not happy with the audio and wish to rerecord, on the Add/Replace tab, click the **Record** button again and rerecord the audio. When finished, click the **Save** button and then click the **Close** button.

2. On the Filmstrip, notice that the thumbnail for slide 2 contains a tiny speaker icon, an indication that audio has been added to the slide.

3. Preview the project.

   Notice that when you get to slide 2, the background audio lowers automatically, and you can hear your narration.

4. Close the preview

5. Save and close the project.

Slide Audio

You've now learned that you can add audio to a slide object (page 145), add background audio to the entire project (page 147), and record your own audio (page 152). Now let's import audio directly to a slide.

Guided Activity 54: Import Audio Onto a Slide

1. Open the **EditMyAudio** project from the **Captivate2019Data** folder.

   This file is similar to the file you were just working on.

2. Import a prerecorded voice narration onto slide 2.

   ☐ on the Filmstrip, select slide **2**

   ☐ choose **Audio > Import to > Slide**

   ☐ from the **Captivate2019Data > audio** folder, open **EditMyAudio.wav**

   Because the audio file you are importing plays longer than the slide, the **Audio Import Options** dialog box opens. You have three options: make the slide timing match the length of the imported audio, force the audio to play over multiple slides, or split the audio equally among all of the slides in the project.

   ☐ ensure **Show the slide for the same amount of time as the length of the audio file** is selected

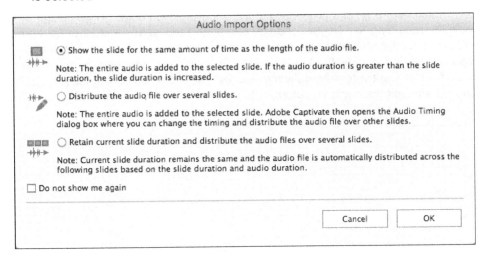

   ☐ click the **OK** button

   You can confirm that audio has been added to the slide via the **speaker icon** that appears in the lower right of the **slide thumbnail** on the **Filmstrip**.

3. Preview the imported slide audio.

    ☐ on the Filmstrip, click the audio icon on slide **2**

    ☐ choose **Play**

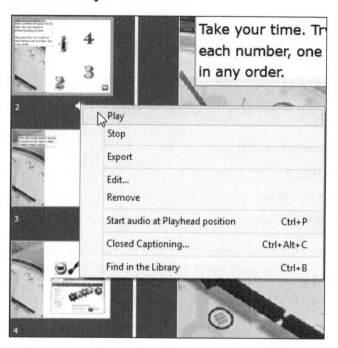

You should hear a bit of a problem with the imported slide audio. The narrator did not know the recording had begun, and you can hear a few gaffes and other background noises. To fix the problems, you can open the original audio file in an audio editing program (like Adobe Audition), edit and repair the issues, and then re-import the edited audio file into Captivate. Alternatively, you can use the audio editing features built within Captivate to edit the audio waveform without ever leaving Captivate. You will do that next.

Guided Activity 55: Edit an Audio File

1. Ensure that the **EditMyAudio** project is still open and that you are on the second slide.

2. Edit an audio clip.

   ☐ still working on slide 2, choose **Audio > Edit > Slide**

   The Slide Audio dialog box opens. There are three tabs (Add/Replace, Edit, and Closed Captioning). You should be on the **Edit** tab.

3. Identify and select the problem areas of the waveform.

   ☐ from the top, center of the dialog box, drag the zoom slider **left** to zoom away from the waveform

   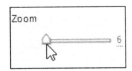

   Your goal is to delete the parts of the waveform that are bad while leaving the good parts alone. The best way to proceed is to select a single segment of the waveform, listen to it, ensure it's not something you want to keep, and then delete it.

   ☐ starting at the **far left** of the waveform, drag **right** to select the first **00:13** seconds of the audio (you can confirm you have selected 13 seconds worth of audio via the Selected area at the bottom right of the waveform)

   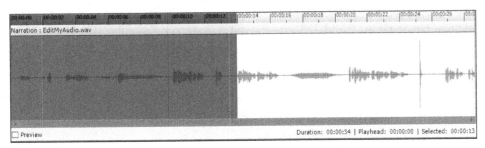

   ☐ click the **Play/Pause** button

   The selected 13 seconds of audio is junk and needs to be removed.

4. Delete the audio gaffe.

   ☐ click the **Delete** button

   And just like that, the selected portion of the audio is gone.

   ☐ click the **Play/Pause** button again [▶] to hear the remaining audio

   There are still some problem areas in the audio. However, with the first 13 seconds deleted, the remaining audio is much better.

   ☐ click the **Save** button and then click the **Close** button

NOTES

Slide Audio Confidence Check

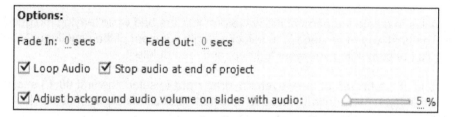

1. Edit the slide audio again. This time, delete the gaffe at the end of the waveform (the last few seconds where the narrator says she's glad the recording is over).

   There are a few more issues with this audio file, but you'll fix those later.

2. Click the **Save** button.

3. Click the **Close** button.

4. Go to slide **3**, and import the **MoveMousePointer.wav** audio to the slide.

5. Preview the project to hear the audio you've added to the project.

   The background audio is too loud, making it difficult to hear the narrator on slides 2 and 3. You'll fix that next.

6. Lower the background audio to something close to **5%** (**Audio > Edit > Background > Add/Replace** tab).

Options:
Fade In: 0 secs   Fade Out: 0 secs
☑ Loop Audio ☑ Stop audio at end of project
☑ Adjust background audio volume on slides with audio: 5 %

7. Preview the project again. Hopefully, this time the background music won't hinder the slide audio on slides 2 and 3. There are still a few issues with the slide audio, but you'll fix those soon enough.

8. Choose **Audio > Audio Management**.

   You can use the Audio Management dialog box to review the audio being used on every object on every slide, play the audio, and/or delete the audio.

9. Select **Show object level audio** (at the bottom left of the dialog box) to see a listing of every audio file used in the project.

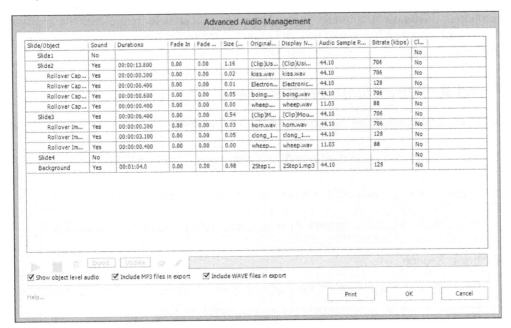

Slide/Object	Sound	Durations	Fade In	Fade ...	Size (...	Original...	Display N...	Audio Sample R...	Bitrate (kbps)	Cl...	
Slide1	No									No	
Slide2	Yes	00:00:13.800	0.00	0.00	1.16	(Clip)Us...	(Clip)Usi...	44.10	706	No	
Rollover Cap...	Yes	00:00:00.300	0.00	0.00	0.02	kiss.wav	kiss.wav	44.10	706	No	
Rollover Cap...	Yes	00:00:00.400	0.00	0.00	0.01	Electron...	Electronic...	44.10	128	No	
Rollover Cap...	Yes	00:00:00.600	0.00	0.00	0.05	boing....	boing.wav	44.10	706	No	
Rollover Cap...	Yes	00:00:00.400	0.00	0.00	0.00	wheep....	wheep.wav	11.03	88	No	
Slide3	Yes	00:00:06.400	0.00	0.00	0.54	(Clip)M...	(Clip)Mou...	44.10	706	No	
Rollover Im...	Yes	00:00:00.300	0.00	0.00	0.03	horn.wav	horn.wav	44.10	706	No	
Rollover Im...	Yes	00:00:03.100	0.00	0.00	0.05	clong_1...	clong_1....	44.10	128	No	
Rollover Im...	Yes	00:00:00.400	0.00	0.00	0.00	wheep....	wheep.wav	11.03	88	No	
Slide4	No									No	
Background	Yes	00:01:04.0	0.00	0.00	0.98	2Step1...	2Step1.mp3	44.10	128	No	

☑ Show object level audio   ☑ Include MP3 files in export   ☑ Include WAVE files in export

Help...   Print   OK   Cancel

10. Select any audio file you like and click the **Export** button at the bottom of the dialog box.

    You can now specify a folder and export any audio file from your project. This is an especially useful feature if you have recorded audio files directly in Captivate, have edited them, and then need to use them in other programs.

11. Cancel the export.

12. Cancel the Advanced Audio Management dialog box.

13. Save and close the project.

Silence

If you come across audio gaffes between waves in your waveform, it may not always be appropriate to delete them. Sometimes deleting parts of a waveform shortens the segments between two waves and has a negative effect on the timing for the rest of the audio. In those instances, it's a better idea to convert the gaffes into silence.

Guided Activity 56: Insert Silence

1. Open **SilenceMe** from the **Captivate2019Data** folder.

2. Go to slide **2** and open the Slide Audio dialog box. (**Audio > Edit > Slide**)

3. Click at the beginning of the waveform and then click the **Play/Pause** button.

   When you get to the 3-second mark, you can hear some pretty bad feedback.

4. Insert Silence.

   ❏ using your mouse, select the part of the waveform representing the feedback

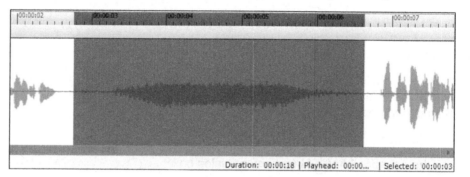

   ❏ at the top of the dialog box, click the **Insert Silence** command

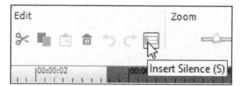

   The audio feedback... gone!

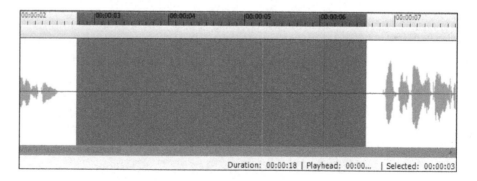

Edit Audio Confidence Check

1. There is a sharp "clap" sound near the 11-second mark. Replace it with silence.

   Now that you have replaced the "clap" sound with silence, return to where you earlier replaced the feedback noise with silence. There should be four full seconds of "dead air" near the 2-second mark on the waveform.

2. Highlight and delete approximately two-thirds of the "dead air" (leave one second of "dead air" so you leave a comfortable pause between the waves).

3. Edit the rest of the waveform and remove the remaining "dead air" so that there isn't more than one second of "dead air" between any segment.

4. Click the **Save** button, and click the **Close** button.

5. Preview the project.

6. When finished, save the project.

NOTES

Text-to-Speech

Artificial voices have been around for years. In fact, there are many applications that allow you to select text and then have text-to-speech software convert the selected text into an audio file. The problem with artificial voices used to be that the voices sounded artificial. Today's text-to-speech technology has made huge strides. Although not perfect, the text-to-speech voices sound more natural than ever before.

Why consider text-to-speech over recorded audio? If you record the audio yourself, you should budget several hours to record the audio and then to *clean* it up (remove lip smacks, other unwanted sounds, and static). In spite of your best efforts, the audio files you create might still be considered less than adequate. And consider the fact that your voice changes over the day. If you need to replace a small segment of a waveform, you will find it challenging to match the audio levels without sophisticated and expensive audio equipment. By using text-to-speech, you can ensure that the audio levels and quality are always consistent. And text-to-speech never gets sick, never takes a vacation, and never asks for compensation.

> **Note:** Before you can take full advantage of Captivate's text-to-speech voices, you need to install the NeoSpeech software. If you have not yet installed NeoSpeech, choose **Audio > Speech Management** and click the link at the bottom of the dialog box. The link takes you to a download page on Adobe's website. You will need to restart Captivate after installing NeoSpeech.

Guided Activity 57: Convert Text-to-Speech

1. Ensure that the **SilenceMe** project is still open.

2. Add Text-to-speech.

   ☐ choose **Audio > Speech Management**

   The Speech Management dialog box opens.

   ☐ from the list of slide, select **Slide 4**

   ☐ click **Add Text-to-speech**

   ☐ type: **This concludes the lesson. Click the images on this screen to visit our website, send us email, or get social with us.**

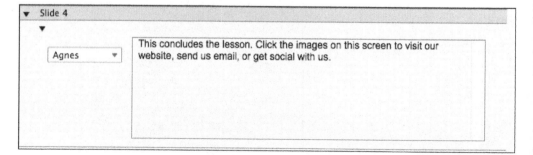

3. Select a Speech Agent.

   ❏ at the left of the text you just typed, click the drop-down menu displaying the current agent's name

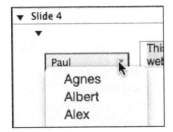

   ❏ choose **any agent** you like

   Note: If you've installed NeoSpeech, Captivate comes with seven voices: Bridget, Chloe, James, Julie, Kate, Paul, and Yumi. Any other voices in your list were installed by some other application (or came with your computer). For instance, both Windows and the Mac OS include voices that serve as assistive devices for the visually impaired. The Macintosh comes with a bunch of voices including Hysterical and Zarvox (both are fun but not ideal Speech Agents). The NeoSpeech agents typically offer higher quality voices than those that ship standard on most computers.

   ❏ click the **Generate Audio** button

   Generate Audio

   ❏ click the **Close** button

4. Preview the project.

   When you get to slide 4, you hear your new text-to-speech audio narration.

5. Save and close the project.

Text-to-Speech Confidence Check

1. Open the **PhotoshopVignette** project from the **Captivate2019Data** folder.

2. Preview the project.

3. Notice that there is background audio playing throughout the project.

4. Notice that there is voice-over audio on most of the slides. The voice-over was created using the text-to-speech feature that you just learned how to use.

5. Close the project (no need to save if prompted).

6. Open the **AddAudioToMe** project from the **Captivate2019Data** folder.

   This project is identical to the **PhotoshopVignette** project—except there isn't any audio.

7. Import the **BeethovenSymphony9.mp3** audio to the background. (Need help? See page 147.)

8. Display the **Slide Notes** panel (Window menu).

9. Most of the slides include Slide Notes. Using any Speech Agent you like, use the Text-to-Speech feature to convert the notes on each slide to audio. (Need help? See page 162.)

   Note: Locate the **TTS** tool in the **Slide Notes** panel on any slide. You can make quick work out of converting text to speech by clicking the check mark just below the TTS tool. Do this for every slide throughout the project. After you've clicked the TTS check box, choose **Audio > Speech Management, Slide notes**. You can use the dialog box to quickly convert the slides notes to speech.

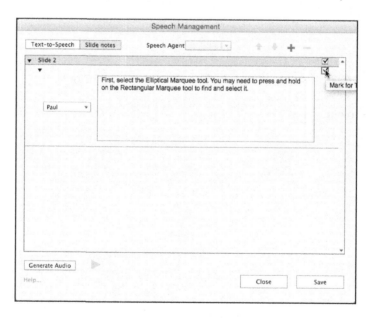

10. Save and close the project.

iCONLOGiC
"Skills and Drills" Learning

Module 9: States, Animations, and Object Effects

In This Module You Will Learn About:

And You Will Learn To:

Object States

By default, an interactive object (such as a button) has three states (or appearances): **Normal**, the way a button looks when it hasn't been clicked; **Rollover**, the way a button looks when the learner hovers above it with the mouse; and **Down**, the way the button looks as it is being clicked by the learner. In the activities that follow, you will learn how to use Captivate's State View to change the appearance of each of the default States.

Guided Activity 58: Change State Views for a Button

1. Open **AnimateMe** from the Captivate2019Data folder.

2. Starting on slide **1**, preview the **Next 5 slides**.

3. Hover above the button on slide **1** and notice that while the button seems to be interactive, the appearance of the button does not change as you hover above it.

4. Click the button and notice that, while you go to the next slide as expected, there is little change to the appearance of the button when it is clicked.

5. Close the preview.

6. Select the button on slide **1** and, on the **Properties Inspector**, **Style Name** area, notice that the button is using a style named **BeginButton**.

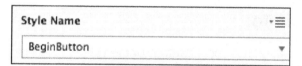

7. Change State Views.

   ☐ with the button on slide **1** still selected, click the **State View** button (near the top of the Properties Inspector)

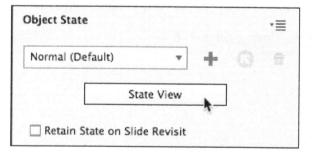

The Filmstrip at the left is replaced with the Object State panel.

   ☐ on the **Object State** panel, select the **RollOver** thumbnail

   ☐ on the **Properties Inspector**, change the Fill and Stroke colors as you see fit

   ☐ on the **Object State** panel, select the **Down** thumbnail

   ☐ on the **Properties Inspector**, change the **Fill** and **Stroke** colors as you see fit

8. Exit State View.

   ☐ at the top of the Captivate window, click **Exit State**

9. Save changes to an existing Object Style.

   ☐ select the button on slide **1** and, on the **Properties Inspector**, **Style Name** area, notice that the button style has a plus sign (meaning the changes that you just made to the appearance of the button's State's have not been added to the Style).

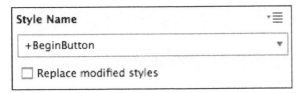

   ☐ from the menu at the right of Style Name, choose **Save changes to Existing Style**

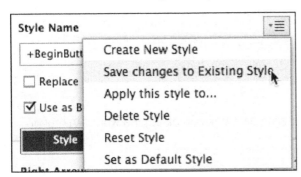

10. Starting on slide **1**, preview the **Next 5 slides**.

11. Hover above the button on slide **1** and notice that the appearance of the button changes to your edited **RollOver** state.

12. Click the button and notice that the appearance of the button changes to your edited **Down** state.

13. Close the preview.

Animations

You can import animations in either the Flash (SWF) or Animated GIF (GIF) format. If you have the time, software, and ability, you can create your own animations and import them into Captivate. You can also search the web for animations. However, if you go the web route, check for copyright restrictions on the animations you find. Captivate comes with several animations, which are in the **SWF Animation** folder (within the Captivate application **Gallery** folder).

> **Note:** As with Rollover Captions (page 142), SWF Animations are not HTML5-compliant and should not be included in your projects if you plan to support mobile learners and/or publish as HTML5.

Guided Activity 59: Add an Animation to a slide

1. Ensure that the **AnimateMe** project is open.

2. Insert an animation.

   ❑ ensure you're on slide **1** and choose **Media > Animation**

   You should automatically be browsing Captivate's **SWF Animation** folder. If not, navigate to the folder where Captivate is installed (typically Program Files/Adobe/Adobe Captivate 2019/Gallery/SWF Animation on Windows; Go > Applications/Adobe Captivate 2019/Gallery/SWF Animation on a Macintosh).

   ❑ open the **Arrows** folder

   ❑ open the **Blue Fade** folder

   ❑ open **downright.swf**

   The animation shows up on your slide as a box containing the word "Animation."

   Next, you will change the animation's slide position and timing.

3. Save your work.

Animations Confidence Check

1. Drag the Animation to the button at the bottom right of the slide until the position of the Animation is similar to the image below.

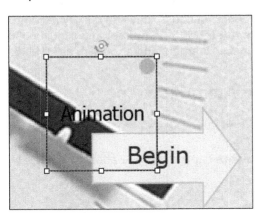

2. Preview the Next 5 slides and notice that the timing of the animation needs work. It would be better if the animation stays around longer (as it is, it appears and goes away so fast you likely missed it). Specifically, you need to have the animation appear after a few seconds and then stick around for the duration of the slide.

3. Close the preview.

4. With the animation selected, use the **Timing Inspector** to change the **Display For** time for the animation to **Rest of Slide**.

5. Change the Appear After to **2.5** sec.

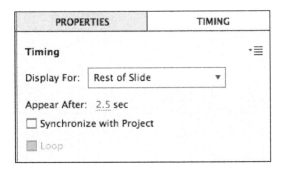

6. From the **Transition** area, change the Transition to **No Transition**.

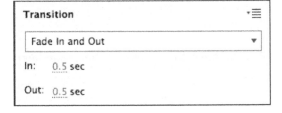

7. Preview the Next 5 slides and notice that the timing of the animation is much improved.

8. Save your work (keep the project open for the next activity).

NOTES

Text Animations

There are more than 90 Text Animations that come with Captivate. Although Text Animations are actually Flash objects, you don't have to own Flash or know how to use Flash to work with Text Animations. Text Animations are typically used to bring text to life. And although they are cool, I would recommend you use Text Animations sparingly because they can quickly become a distraction. Most important, Text Animations **are not HTML5-compliant** and should not be included in your projects if you plan to support mobile learners and/or publish as HTML5.

Guided Activity 60: Insert a Text Animation

1. Ensure that the **AnimateMe** project is still open.

2. On slide **1**, delete the **Creating New Folders** caption. (You're about to insert a text animation in its place.)

3. Insert Text Animation.

   ❏ still working on slide **1**, choose **Text > Text Animation**

   The Text Animation Properties dialog box appears.

   ❏ replace the words **Sample Text** with **Creating New Folders**

   ❏ change the **Font** to **Verdana** and the Size to **34**

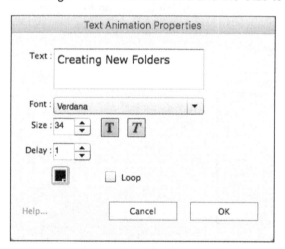

   ❏ click the **OK** button

   The animation appears on the slide.

   ❏ reposition the text animation until its slide position is similar to the image below

---

4. Change animation effects.

❏ with the text animation selected, go to the **Properties Inspector**

❏ from the **Effect** drop-down menu, choose **Red_Hot_Skew**

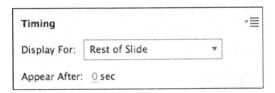

| Effect | Red_Hot_Skew ▼ |

You see a sample of the effect at the top of the Properties Inspector.

❏ from the **Effect** drop-down menu, choose **Twinkle**

Once again, you see a sample of the effect in the area at the top of the Properties Inspector.

Text Animation Confidence Check

1. Using the Timing Inspector, change the **Display For** to **Rest of Slide**.

Timing	⋮≡
Display For:	Rest of Slide ▼
Appear After:	0 sec

2. From the Transition area, change the Transition to **No Transition**.

| Transition | ⋮≡ |
| No Transition ▼ | |

3. Preview the Next 5 slides to see the text animation in action.

4. When finished, close the preview.

5. Save your work and then close the project.

NOTES

Object Effects

Similar to Microsoft PowerPoint's powerful animation features, you can also apply animation effects to selected slide objects without ever leaving Captivate. Using the Properties Inspector, you can apply a single animation effect to one object or several. And you can tightly control such effect options as timing and direction.

Guided Activity 61: Apply an Effect to a Slide Object

1. Open **EffectMe** from the **Captivate2019Data** folder.

2. Go to slide **2**.

   There are four text captions on the slide. You are about to apply two effects to the "During this demonstration..." caption.

3. Apply a Fly-In Effect to a Text Caption.

   ☐ select the text caption containing the words "During this demonstration..."

   ☐ on the **Timing Inspector**, **Effects** area, click the drop-down menu currently displaying **Basic** and choose **Entrance**

   ☐ from the bottom of the **Entrance Effects,** click **>** and choose **Fly in From Right**

On the **Timing Inspector**, the Effect has been added to the Applied Effects List. If you need to delete the Effect, you can click the **Trash** icon to the right of the Applied Effects List drop-down menu.

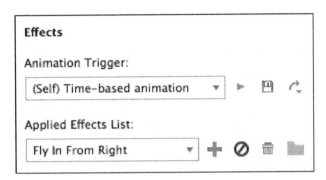

On the slide, notice that an FX has appeared in the upper right of the selected Text Caption. In addition, there's a red line starting on the Pasteboard and ending up on the caption.

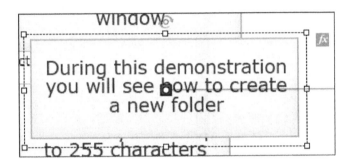

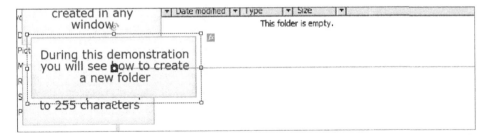

4. Preview the Next 5 slides.

    The text caption appears from the right side of the screen and stops in its original slide position.

5. Close the Preview and then save your work.

Guided Activity 62: Apply a Free Fall Effect to an Object

1. Ensure that the **EffectMe** project is still open.

2. Apply a Emphasis Effect to a Text Caption.

   ☐ ensure that the "During this demonstration..." caption is still selected,

   ☐ on the **Timing Inspector**, **Effects** area, click **Add Effect**

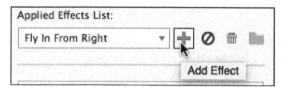

   ☐ from the **Effects** area, choose **Emphasis** from the drop-down menu

   ☐ from the **Emphasis Effects**, choose **Free Fall**

3. Preview the Effects.

   ☐ choose **Preview > Play Slide**

   Both Effects work, but they occur at the same time. During the next activity you'll control the timing of both effects.

Guided Activity 63: Edit Effects Timing

1. Ensure that the **EffectMe** project is still open.

2. Change the timing for an Effect.

   ☐ on the **Timeline**, click the **arrow** to the **left** of the **During this demonstration** caption

   You can see the two Effects you've added to the caption.

   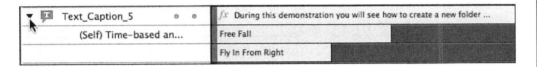

   ☐ drag the Free Fall effect right until its right edge lines up with the right edge of the **During this demonstration** caption

   ☐ drag the left edge of the Free Fall Effect a bit to the right (to shorten the playtime of the Effect similar to the image below)

   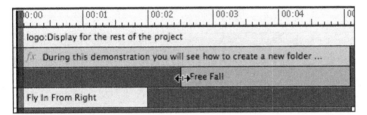

3. Save your work.

4. Play the Slide.

   The caption flies in from the right and stops. Then the Free Fall effect kicks in until the caption disappears off of the bottom of the slide.

5. Save your work and then close the project.

Notes

iCONLOGiC

"Skills and Drills" Learning

Module 10: Software Simulations

In This Module You Will Learn About:

- Demonstrations versus Simulations, page 178
- Find and Replace, page 179
- Click Boxes, page 181
- Text Entry Boxes, page 185

And You Will Learn To:

- Hide the Mouse, page 178
- Replace Phrases, page 179
- Insert a Click Box, page 181
- Insert a Text Entry Box, page 185

Demonstrations versus Simulations

The most common types of eLearning lessons that developers create with Captivate are soft skills training, software demonstrations, software simulations, and Video Demos. At the beginning of this book, you learned how to create a soft skills lesson from scratch (page 23). You then learned how to record actions and create software demonstrations and interactive simulations (beginning on page 46). After that, you tackled Video Demos (page 66).

Earlier in this book (beginning on page 86) you worked on producing software demonstrations—projects that are intended to demonstrate actions taken on a computer. Although you added some interactivity to a project when you learned about buttons, the project did not necessarily encourage learner interaction. Learners watching a demonstration would be expected to merely sit back and watch slide objects appear on the screen and watch the mouse move around the slide. Although there is nothing wrong with software demonstrations, software simulations can improve the learning experience by letting users actively participate in the lesson.

Most people who teach themselves Captivate produce mostly software demonstrations. Why? The most common reasons I hear are (1) I didn't know how to create a simulation and (2) I thought creating a simulation would be too hard. After this module, you will know how to quickly take an existing software demonstration and convert it into a software simulation.

Guided Activity 64: Hide the Mouse

1. Open **ConvertMeToSimulation** from the **Captivate2019Data** folder.

   On the Filmstrip, notice that there is a mouse icon in the lower right of slides **3** through **9**. The mouse icon is a visual indicator that the mouse pointer is appearing on the slide. This demonstration project has been saved with a new name so that it can be converted into a simulation. One step to converting a demonstration into a simulation is to hide the mouse.

2. Hide the mouse for slides 3 through 9.

   ☐ on the **Filmstrip**, select slides **3** through **9**

   Note: One way to select the range of slides is to select slide **3**, press [**Shift**] on your keyboard, and then click one time on slide **9**.

   ☐ choose **Modify > Mouse > Show Mouse** (to turn the Show Mouse command off)

   The image at the left shows slide 3 with the mouse icon in the lower right of the slide thumbnail. The second image is missing the mouse icon.

Find and Replace

Although you can use Captivate's Find and Replace feature to find any object in your project (including images, animation, and Flash video), this feature is most useful for quickly replacing words or phrases throughout a project. During the following activity, you will use Captivate's Find and Replace feature to replace phrases to make the lesson more action oriented.

Guided Activity 65: Replace Phrases

1. Ensure that the ConvertMeToSimulation project is still open.

2. Go to slide **3**.

   Notice that the text in the Text Caption (**Watch as the File menu is selected**) as written does not encourage the learner to interact with the lesson. The learner is being encouraged to simply "watch" as something happens. You'll use the Find and Replace feature to replace the phrase "Watch as" with "Select."

3. Replace a phrase.

   ☐ choose **Edit > Find and Replace**

   The Find and Replace window opens.

   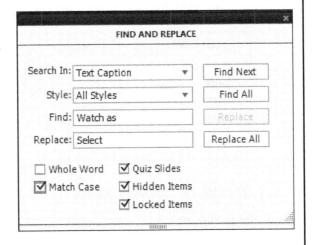

   ☐ from the **Search In** drop-down menu, ensure **Text Caption** is selected

   ☐ from the **Style** drop-down menu, ensure that **All Styles** is selected

   ☐ in the **Find** field, type **Watch as**

   ☐ in the **Replace** field, type **Select**

   ☐ from the lower left of the panel select **Match Case**

   Ensure that you typed both entries exactly as written above and have matched the case.

   ☐ click the **Find Next** button

   The first caption containing the phrase you typed into the Find field is selected.

   ☐ click the **Replace All** button

   You are alerted that four instances of the phrase have been found and replaced.

   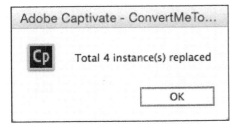

   ☐ click the **OK** button

Find and Replace Confidence Check

1. Use the Find and Replace feature to delete the phrase **is selected** from all of the Text Captions.

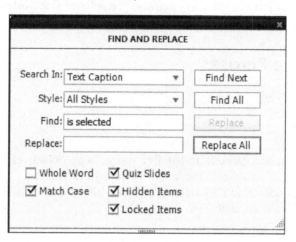

You should be alerted of four more changes to the project.

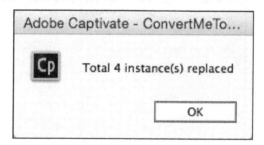

2. Close the Find and Replace panel.

3. Save your work.

Click Boxes

Instead of telling and then showing a learner how to perform an action, you can insert Click Boxes that allow the learner to perform actions, such as clicking a menu or menu command.

Guided Activity 66: Insert a Click Box

1. Ensure that the **ConvertMeToSimulation** project is still open.

2. Preview the project.

   There is an interactive button on the first slide. Clicking the button takes you to slide 2. From this point forward, there is no interactivity in the project.

3. Close the preview.

4. Insert a Click Box on slide **3**.

   ☐ go to slide **3**

   ☐ choose **Interactions > Click Box**

   A new Click Box appears in the middle of your screen. The mouse badge on the lower right of the Click Box, although small, contains valuable information. If you look closely, you see a green icon on the top left side of the mouse badge indicating that the Click Box is activated with a left click. You can use the Click Box Properties to set the box to be right clickable by your learners, in which case the right side of the mouse badge is red.

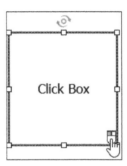

5. Confirm the On Success action and Attempts settings for the Click Box.

   ☐ double-click the newly inserted Click Box

   ☐ on the **Properties Inspector**, select the **Actions** tab

   ☐ from the **On Success** drop-down menu, ensure **Go to the next slide** is selected

   Using this Action, the learner immediately is taken to slide 4 when the Click Box is clicked.

   ☐ ensure that **Infinite Attempts** is selected

   Using this option, a learner can click outside of the Click Box again and again. However, the **Go to the next slide** action does not occur until the learner successfully clicks the Click Box.

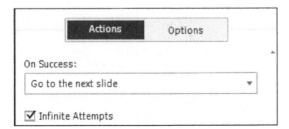

6. Add a Failure Caption to the Click Box.

    ☐ still working on the **Properties Inspector**, **Display** area, select **Failure**

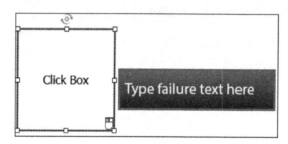

A Failure caption appears on the slide along with the Click Box. This is what learners see when they click anywhere on the slide except the Click Box.

Note: The **Pause for Success/Failure Captions** option you see in the **Others** area ensures that the learner is given a chance to read the Failure Caption before getting frustrated and clicking again in the wrong place. The **Disable Click Sound** option ensures that the learners don't hear a double-click sound when they click the Click Box (their click and one created by the Click Box). And **Pause project until user clicks** ensures that the lesson does not continue unless the learner interacts with the Click Box.

7. Reposition the Click Box.

    ☐ **drag** the Click Box **up** and to the **left** and resize it so that it covers the word "File" in the File menu on the slide background

8. Position the Failure Caption on the slide.

    ☐ position the Failure Caption to the right of the Click Box

9. Edit the Failure Caption's text.

☐ right-click the Failure Caption and choose **Edit Text**

☐ replace the text with **Ooops. You need to select the File menu.**

Your screen should look similar to the image below.

NOTES

Click Boxes Confidence Check

1. Preview the project from slide 3.

2. Test the Failure Caption by clicking anywhere except the File menu.

3. Close the Preview.

4. Go to slide **5**.

5. Insert a Click Box over the **New** command on the slide. The Click Box should take learners to the **next slide** when they click it.

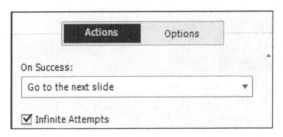

6. Edit the Failure Caption text so that it reads **Sorry but you need to select the New Command**.

7. Position the Click Box over the New command and then resize the Click Box as necessary so it is no larger than the **New** command.

8. Position the Failure Caption so it is similar to the picture below.

9. Insert similar Click Boxes on slides **6** and **8**. (The exact wording you use in the Failure captions is up to you.)

10. When finished, preview the project and test each of the Click Boxes you added.

11. Close the preview.

12. Save and close the project.

Text Entry Boxes

You can use Text Entry Boxes to simulate areas in an application that require a user to type data. Learners can be instructed to type specific information into a Text Entry Box and, depending on what they type, captions can provide the appropriate feedback.

Guided Activity 67: Insert a Text Entry Box

1. Open **PasswordMe** from the **Captivate2019Data** folder.

2. On slide 1, notice that there is a Text Caption instructing the learner to enter a password to take the course. You will create a Text Entry Box that accepts a specific password.

3. Insert a Text Entry Box.

   ☐ choose **Text > Text Entry Box**

   Two objects appear on the slide: a Text Entry Box and a submit button. As with most objects, the appearance of objects is controlled by Object Styles. I have already edited the Object Styles via the Object Style Manager.

   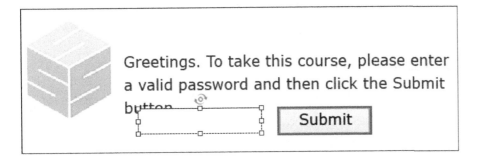

4. Validate User Input.

   ☐ double-click the **Text Entry Box**

   ☐ on the **Properties Inspector**, **Style** tab, select **Validate User Input**

   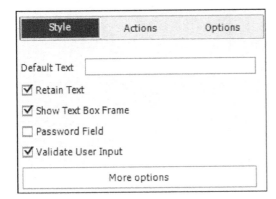

   A **Correct Entries** dialog box appears on the slide. You can now set it up so that there are correct answers associated with the Text Entry Box.

   ☐ in the upper right of the **Correct Entries** dialog box, click the **Plus** sign

NOTES

☐ type **captivate** as the Correct Entry

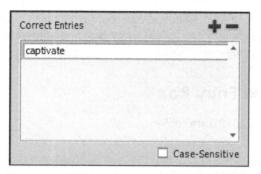

5. Set more Properties for the Text Entry Box.

☐ ensure the Text Entry Box is still selected

☐ on the **Properties Inspector**, **Style** tab, deselect **Retain Text**

With this option deselected, the text a learner types into the Text Entry Box is removed when the learner chooses to rewind and work through the lesson again.

☐ if necessary, select **Show Text Box Frame**

This option ensures that the Text Entry Box is visible to the learner.

☐ select **Password Field**

With this option selected, the text a learner types into the Text Entry Box is replaced with asterisks.

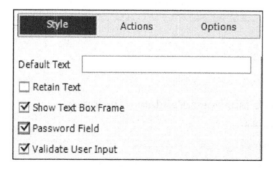

6. Set the Action for the Text Entry Box.

   ❏ ensure the Text Entry Box is still selected

   ❏ select the Actions tab on the Properties Inspector

   ❏ from the On Success drop-down menu, choose **Go to the next slide**

   ❏ ensure that **Infinite Attempts** is selected

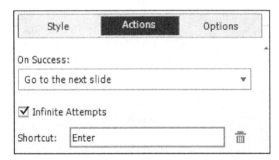

7. Enable a Failure caption.

   ❏ from the Display area, select **Failure**

Text Entry Box Confidence Check

1. Move/resize/edit the screen objects until the slide looks similar to the image below.

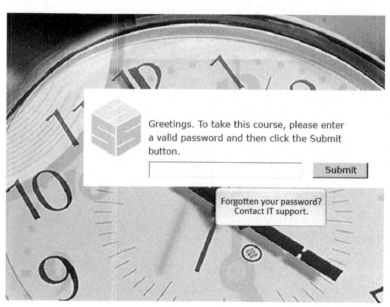

2. Preview the Next 5 slides.

3. Type **Hello** into the Text Entry Box on slide **1** and then click the **Submit** button.

   Because you did not type the text correctly, the Failure Caption appears.

4. Type **captivate** into the box and then click the **Submit** button.

   This time the lesson should continue without incident.

5. Close the preview.

6. Save and close the project.

iCONLOGiC

"Skills and Drills" Learning

Module 11: Working With PowerPoint

In This Module You Will Learn About:

And You Will Learn To:

Starting with PowerPoint

If you or a colleague has already created eLearning course content as a presentation using Microsoft PowerPoint, don't throw it away. You can import the presentation slides into an existing Captivate project or create a new project that uses the PowerPoint slides. During the import process, Captivate creates a link between the Captivate project and the original PowerPoint presentation. Using this work-flow, most changes made to the original PowerPoint presentation can be reflected in the Captivate project.

PowerPoint must be installed on your computer before you can import PowerPoint presentations into Captivate. Additionally, it often helps to have PowerPoint running before you attempt to import a presentation into Captivate, especially on a PC (with PowerPoint running, I tend to see fewer error messages about memory and/or corrupt files such as the one shown below).

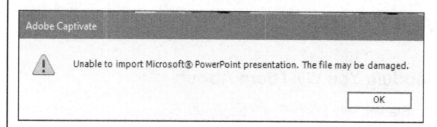

Guided Activity 68: Create a Project from a Presentation

1. Start Microsoft PowerPoint.

2. Create a new Captivate project from a PowerPoint presentation.

   ☐ return to Captivate

   ☐ choose **File > New Project > Project From MS PowerPoint**

   The Open dialog box appears.

   ☐ from the **Captivate2019Data** folder, open **S3_Policies.pptx**

   The **Convert Microsoft PowerPoint Presentations** dialog box opens, offering a few controls over the way the PowerPoint presentation will be imported into Captivate.

   ☐ if the current Width and Height isn't 800 x 600, click the **Preset Sizes** menu and choose **800 x 600**

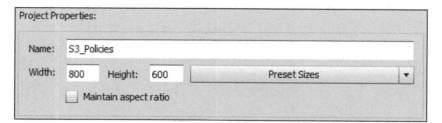

3. Set the PowerPoint to Captivate conversion options.

☐ ensure that **Selected slides: 26/26** appears at the bottom of the dialog box (if not, click the **Select All** button)

☐ from the **Advance Slide** drop-down menu, ensure **On mouse click** is selected

Selected Slides: 26/26	Select All	Clear All

The **On mouse click** option adds a large click box to each slide in the pending Captivate project. The other available option, **Automatically**, results in Captivate slides that continue from slide to slide after a delay of just a few seconds. Between the two options, **On mouse click** is the more common and results in a more interactive eLearning lesson in Captivate.

☐ **Windows users only**, select **High Fidelity** (the option is not available for Mac users)

✔ High Fidelity	✔ Linked	☐ Slide Duration

During a standard import process, PowerPoint pptx presentations are first converted to the ppt format and then converted to SWF. If you select **High Fidelity**, the import process takes native pptx files directly to Captivate SWF (the ppt conversion is skipped). This option, which is available only in Captivate for Windows, results in the best-looking content in Captivate, but it could take a long time to import. (Five minutes or more in some cases.)

☐ all users, ensure **Linked** is selected

The Linked option creates a link between the PowerPoint presentation and the new Captivate project. The link allows you to open the PowerPoint presentation from within Captivate. Additionally, any changes made externally to the PowerPoint presentation can be reflected in the Captivate project with a few simple mouse clicks.

☐ click the **OK** button

Note: If you changed the size of the imported presentation to 800 x 600 (typically it's the Mac users who need to do so), you'll get an alert dialog box that's concerned with the resolution of the resulting Captivate project. If you had changed the size of the project to something larger than the original, resolution might be negatively affected. In this instance, there isn't anything to worry about, so you can click the **Yes** button.

Adobe Captivate

The height and width of the Microsoft PowerPoint presentation and the chosen Adobe Captivate project are not same. This might affect the resolution of the imported slides in Adobe Captivate. But the quality is largely regained on publishing. Continue?

No	Yes

NOTES

The presentation is imported into Adobe Captivate and the PowerPoint slides are added to Captivate's Filmstrip.

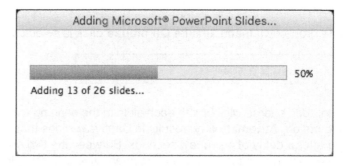

4. Save the project to the **Captivate2019Data** folder as **S3_Policies_Integration**.

5. Preview the project.

   ☐ choose **Preview > Project**

   Because a click box has been added to each of the Captivate slides during the import process, you will need to click your mouse once on each slide to move through the presentation. As I mentioned earlier, I've found that every aspect of PowerPoint that I've tested (hyperlinks, audio, transitions, and animations) continues to work as a Captivate project. I haven't tested everything. If you happen upon a PowerPoint feature that does not work within Captivate, please let me know (email me at ksiegel@iconlogic.com).

6. Close the preview (keep the **S3_Policies_Integration** project open).

Guided Activity 69: Edit a Linked PowerPoint Presentation

1. Ensure that the **S3_Policies_Integration** Captivate project is still open.

2. Edit the slides with PowerPoint.

   ❏ choose **Edit > Edit with Microsoft PowerPoint > Edit Presentation**

   The Captivate slides that originated in PowerPoint open in the original PowerPoint presentation. If you've used PowerPoint before, you recognize the familiar PowerPoint interface. However, if you are using Windows, there are two buttons you wouldn't normally see in PowerPoint: the **Save** and **Cancel** buttons at the upper left of the window. (Although the Save and Cancel buttons do not exist for Mac users, the editing process works just fine.)

   ❏ go to slide **2** of the PowerPoint presentation

   ❏ drag the rocket ship a bit higher on the slide

   ❏ if you'd like, make some other changes (rotate the rocket ship or change its colors)

3. Save the PowerPoint changes and update the Captivate project.

   ❏ Windows users, click the **Save** button in the upper left of the window; Mac users, **Quit** PowerPoint (save when prompted)

   Windows users, the changes you just made to the PowerPoint presentation are saved, the PowerPoint presentation is closed, and the Captivate slides are automatically updated in Captivate. **Mac users**, you are prompted to import the updated presentation (which you should allow by clicking the **Yes** button.

   The changes you made to the PowerPoint file appear in the Captivate project.

NOTES

Apply to All Confidence Check

As mentioned earlier, there is a large click box on every Captivate slide (thanks to the **On Mouse Click** option you selected during the import process you went through on page 190). The click boxes are great because they keep the lesson from moving forward until the learner clicks the click box. However, the click box includes what is often considered an annoying click sound. You'll remove that next.

1. Still working in the **S3_Policies_Integration project,** double-click the middle of any slide to select the slide's click box. (The click box is the same size as the slide.)

2. From the **Actions** tab on the **Properties Inspector, Others** area, select **Disable Click Sound**.

3. Use the menu at the right of the **Display** area to apply your change to **all items of this type**.

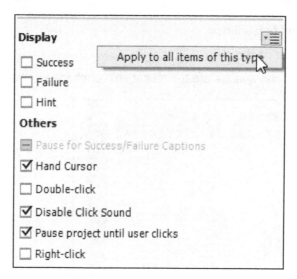

4. Save your work.

5. Preview the project and notice that the click sound has been removed.

6. Close the preview (keep the project open).

PowerPoint Round Tripping

You have just learned that as a Captivate developer, you can import a PowerPoint presentation and, thanks to the Link feature, initiate changes to the PowerPoint presentation from within Captivate. *Nice!* But let's assume that you've imported the presentation from a network drive. A colleague has made changes to the original PowerPoint presentation but has neglected to tell you. If the source PowerPoint presentation is updated, you are able to see that the Captivate project is no longer synchronized with the PowerPoint presentation via the Library, and you can grab the updates.

Guided Activity 70: Synchronize With Source

1. Minimize (Hide) Captivate, and open the **S3_Policies** presentation directly in PowerPoint.

2. Edit the slides with PowerPoint.

   ☐ using PowerPoint, open the **S3_Policies** presentation (the presentation is in the **Captivate2019Data** folder)

   ☐ on slide 1, change the **&** to the word **AND**

3. Save the presentation and exit (quit) PowerPoint.

4. Return to Captivate. (The **S3_Policies_Integration** project should still be open.)

5. On slide **1** of the Captivate project, notice that the edit made externally to the PowerPoint presentation does not appear on the corresponding Captivate slide.

   You will next update the Captivate project with the change you made in the PowerPoint presentation.

NOTES

6. Open the Library.

   ☐ at the far right of the Captivate window, click **Library**

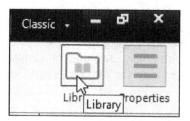

On the Library, notice that there is a **Status** column (you may need to resize the other Library columns to see the Status column). The red bullet indicates that the S3_Policies presentation within the Captivate project is no longer synchronized with the PowerPoint presentation. (The changes you just made to the presentation have not yet been reflected in the Captivate project.)

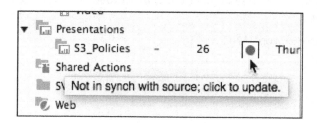

7. Synchronize with source.

   ☐ click the **Red** bullet

The edited PowerPoint slides are updated in the Captivate project. On the Library, the color of the button in the Status column changes from red to green.

Note: Be patient as the update process progresses. Depending on the speed of your computer, the process could take a few moments.

8. On slide **1** of the Captivate project, notice that the edit you made in the PowerPoint presentation appears in Captivate.

9. Save your work.

Note: If you no longer want the PowerPoint presentation in your project to be linked to the original PowerPoint presentation, you can **embed** the presentation in your project. On the Library, right-click the presentation and choose **Change to Embedded**. Once embedded, the size of your Captivate project increases significantly and you are no longer able to receive updates from the original PowerPoint presentation. If you change your mind, you can restore the link to the original presentation by right-clicking the presentation on the Library and choosing **Change to Linked**.

Rescaling Projects

If your project was recorded at a specific size and you now need it to be bigger or smaller, you can use Captivate's **Rescale project** command to quickly resize it—a real time saver over having to rerecord the entire lesson. When you rescale the project, you can instruct Captivate to ensure that the project's captions are rescaled if the resized project is smaller than the original.

> **Note:** You will not be able to use the Undo command to undo a rescale. Also, if you rescale a project, you could degrade the visual quality of the project.

Guided Activity 71: Rescale a Project

1. Ensure that the **S3_Policies_Integration** project is still open.

2. Rename the project.

   ❑ choose **File > Save As**, change the name to **S3_Policies_Integration_Resized**, and save it to the **Captivate2019Data** folder

3. Rescale a project larger.

   ❑ choose **Modify > Rescale project**

   The Rescale Project dialog box appears.

   ❑ in the **Size** area, ensure that **Maintain Aspect Ratio** is selected

   ❑ change the **Width** to **1200** and press [**tab**]

   Once you leave the Width field, the Height should automatically become **900** (thanks to the **Maintain Aspect Ratio** option).

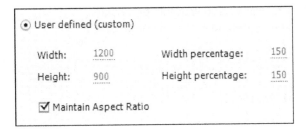

   ❑ from the **If new size is larger** area, select **Rescale Project to Fit New Size** (if necessary)

   ❑ ensure that **Rescale all Objects** is selected

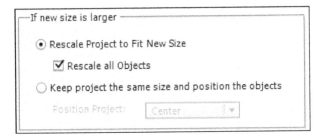

Although just about everything in the project comes directly from the PowerPoint presentation, there are click boxes on every slide. Thanks to the Rescale options, each of those click boxes is going to resize proportionally to the new size of the project.

☐ click the **Finish** button

A warning appears. As mentioned earlier, you cannot undo this step. However, if you are not satisfied with the results, you can close the project without saving.

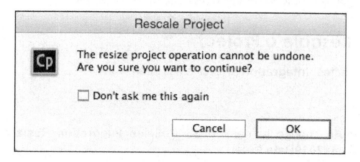

☐ click the **OK** button

The project's slides are now much larger.

Rescaling Confidence Check

1. Preview the project.

2. As you move from slide to slide, notice that the quality of the slides is actually quite good (astonishing, considering that you rescaled the project to make it significantly larger).

   Note: Although the quality of the rescale worked with this particular project, keep in mind that rescaling may lead to a loss of image quality in other projects.

3. Close the preview.

4. Close the project (there is no need to save it).

iCONLOGiC

"Skills and Drills" Learning

Module 12: Quizzing

In This Module You Will Learn About:

And You Will Learn To:

Quiz Setup

You will soon be adding a few question slides to an existing Captivate project. Before proceeding, it's a good idea to set up a few things that will make the process of creating a quiz a bit more efficient. For instance, if you set up the Object Styles for the Quiz objects, the fonts on the question slides will look consistent throughout the project. In addition, you should set some basic Quiz Preferences to control such things as general quiz navigation and the Pass/Fail options.

Guided Activity 72: Edit Quizzing Object Styles

1. Open **QuizMe** from the **Captivate2019Data** folder.

2. Use the Object Style Manager to set the formatting for Quizzing Objects.

    ☐ choose **Edit > Object Style Manager**

    ☐ at the upper left of the Object Style Manager dialog box, expand the **Quizzing Objects**

    ☐ expand the **Captions**

    ☐ from the list of captions, select **Correct Caption**

    ☐ at the right side of the dialog box, from the **Text Format** area, change the **Family** to **Calibri**

    Note: If Calibri is not available in your list of fonts, use **Tahoma** instead. (While Calibri is a standard, web safe font, I've seen some systems—typically Macs—where Calibri is missing for whatever reason.)

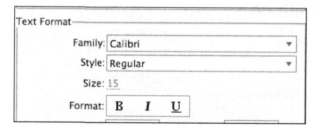

3. Review some of the other Quizzing Object styles.

    ☐ from the **Quizzing Objects** area, select any of the remaining objects

    To save you time, I have already formatted the remaining styles so they use consistent fonts, sizes, etc.

    ☐ click the **OK** button

Guided Activity 73: Set the Quiz Preferences

1. Ensure that the **QuizMe** project is still open.

2. Set the Quiz Preferences.

   ☐ choose **Quiz > Quiz Preferences**

   The Preferences dialog box opens.

   ☐ from the **Quiz** category at the left, select **Settings**

   ☐ from the **Quiz** area, change the Name of the Quiz to **Safety Quiz**

   ☐ from the Required drop-down menu, select **Answer All - The user must answer every question to continue**

   > **Quiz: Settings**
   >
   > Quiz:
   >
   >   Name: | Safety Quiz |
   >
   >   Required: | Answer All – The user must answer every question... ▼ |

   ☐ from the **Settings** area, ensure your options match the picture below

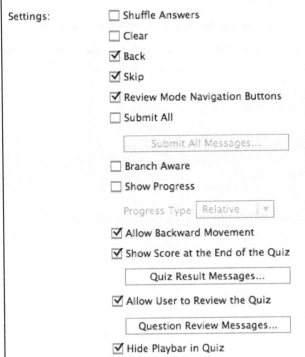

After a learner answers a question in the quiz, the learner needs to be diligent about clicking the slide's **Submit** button before going to the next question. Failure to click the Submit button means that Captivate treats the answer as incorrect, even if the learner selects the correct answer. To prevent learners from accidentally failing to click the Submit button and causing a lot of heartache along the way, Captivate provides a **Submit All** option that would add a Submit All button on each Question Slide instead of a Submit

NOTES

NOTES

button. If the learner answers a question and clicks Next (without clicking Submit All), Captivate allows the learner to go to the next question. However, on the last question, if the learner clicks Next, an alert dialog box opens that encourages the learner to Submit All answers. In this instance, you're going with a Submit button. You'll have a chance to see how Submit All works later in a different project (page 209).

The **Show Progress** option inserts a counter on each Question slide so that learners know where they are in the quiz.

Allow Backward Movement allows learners to go backward through the quiz.

When you select **Show score at the End of the Quiz**, Captivate adds an additional slide to the project that summarizes how learners score on the quiz.

The **Allow User to Review the Quiz** option allows learners to go back and see how they answered the questions. However, once the answers are submitted for scoring, learners are not able to change their answers.

The **Hide Playbar in Quiz** will ensure the project's Playbar does not appear on the Question Slides (providing a way for learners to skip over questions).

Note: I didn't cover all of the options in the Quiz Settings dialog box. You can learn about the other options by clicking the **Help** link at the bottom of the dialog box. You will typically find a Help link in most of Captivate's dialog boxes.

3. Set the Pass or Fail options for the Quiz.

   ☐ from the **Quiz** category at the left of the dialog box, select **Pass or Fail**

   ☐ from the Pass/Fail Options area, change the **% or more of total points to pass** to **50**

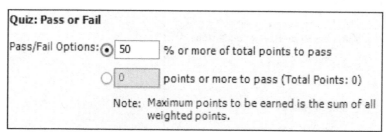

Learners need to correctly answer half of the questions to pass the quiz.

4. Set the Passing and Failing Grade action.

☐ from the **Action** drop-down menu for both **If Passing Grade** and **If Failing Grade**, choose **Go to the next slide**

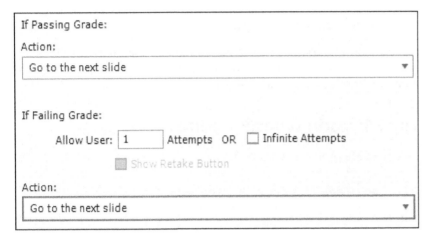

By setting both Actions to **Go to the next slide**, it doesn't matter how learners do on the quiz, they'll end up on next slide on the Filmstrip. You could, however, take learners to a specific slide (or website) should they pass; another should they fail.

☐ click the **OK** button

There should be a new slide in the project: Quiz Results. The slide was created because you selected **Show score at the End of the Quiz**.

5. Reposition the Results slide.

☐ on the **Filmstrip**, drag the Quiz Results slide down and position it above the last slide

Question Slides

Captivate allows you to add nine different types of Question Slides: Multiple Choice, True/False, Fill-in-the-Blank, Short Answer, Matching, Hot Spot, Sequence, Rating Scale (Likert), and Random Question. All of the Question Slides can be graded (worth a specific number of points) except for Rating Scale (Likert), which is typically used for surveys.

Ideally, any eLearning quizzes you create will be short... no more than 5-10 questions. A quiz longer than that is too long and makes your eLearning lesson all about the quiz instead of transferring knowledge from the lesson to your learner.

Guided Activity 74: Insert Question Slides

1. Ensure that the **QuizMe** project is still open.

2. Insert a Multiple Choice and True/False Question slide.

   ☐ select slide **10**

   ☐ choose **Quiz > Question slide**

   The Insert Questions dialog box opens. If you click the Help link in the lower left of the dialog box, you can read more information about the available question types.

   ☐ from the list of Question Types, select **Multiple Choice**

   ☐ in the field to the right of Multiple Choice, type **2**

   ☐ from the drop-down menu to the right of the Question, ensure that **Graded** is selected

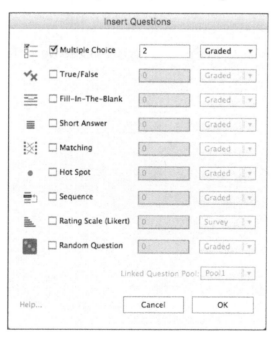

   ☐ click the **OK** button

   Two new slides are added to your project. Both slides contain Multiple Choice questions.

3. Save your work.

Guided Activity 75: Edit a Question Slide

1. Ensure that the **QuizMe** project is still open.

2. Type a Question and set a Point value.

   ☐ go to slide **11**

   ☐ replace the **Type the question here** text with **What is a PPE?**

3. Type two of the Answers.

   ☐ replace the first **type the answer here** with **Personal Protective Equipment**

   ☐ replace the second **type the answer here** with **Prepared Protective Environment**

What is a PPE?

- A) Personal Protective Equipment
- B) Prepared Protective Environment

4. Use the Quiz Inspector to add more answers to the question and change its point value.

   ☐ at the far right of the Captivate window, click the **Quiz Inspector**

   ☐ change the number of **Answers** to **4**

   ☐ change the Points to **50**

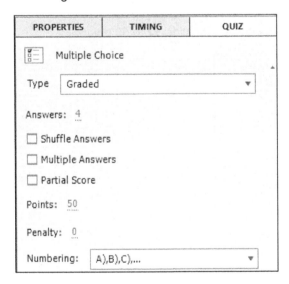

In addition to the question now being worth 50 points, two more answers have been added to the slide.

5. Replace the third "type the answer here" with **Preferred Protective Environment.**

6. Replace the last "type the answer here" with **Profound Prepared Effective.**

7. Specify "A" as the correct answer.

   ☐ if necessary, click in the circle to the left of **A) Personal Protective Equipment** to make it the correct answer

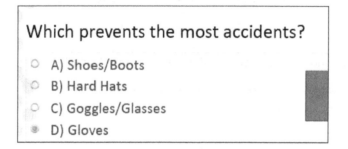

What is a PPE?

- ● A) Personal Protective Equipment
- ○ B) Prepared Protective Environment
- ○ C) Preferred Protective Environment
- ○ D) Profound Prepared Effective

Quiz Confidence Check

1. Edit the True/False question on slide **12** as follows:

Which prevents the most accidents?

- ○ A) Shoes/Boots
- ○ B) Hard Hats
- ○ C) Goggles/Glasses
- ● D) Gloves

2. On the Quiz Inspector, change the Point value for slide **12** to **50** points.

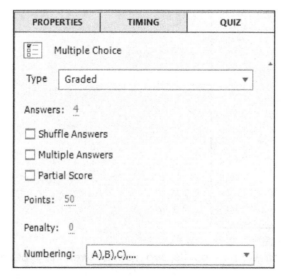

PROPERTIES	TIMING	QUIZ

Multiple Choice

Type Graded ▼

Answers: 4

☐ Shuffle Answers

☐ Multiple Answers

☐ Partial Score

Points: 50

Penalty: 0

Numbering: A),B),C),... ▼

3. Remove the **Back** and **Skip** buttons from both question slides.

4. Preview the project and take the quiz. (Keep in mind that you need to click **Submit** after answering each question.)

5. When finished, close the preview.

6. On slide **12**, notice that there a gray box with white text. This is a feedback caption. There are currently three feedback captions on the slide: Correct, Incorrect, and a reminder to answer. You cannot see the other feedback captions because all three are currently stacked on top of each other.

7. Pull the captions away from each other.

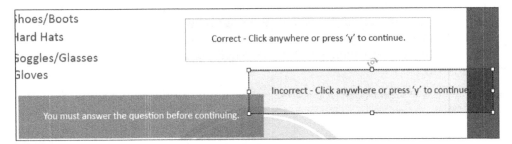

8. If you'd like, edit the incorrect feedback caption. One suggested edit would be, **Sorry, the correct answer is Gloves.**

9. Reposition the feedback captions so they are stacked on top of each other. (One quick way to do this would be to select them all, right-click, and then choose the **Align** menu item.)

10. Beginning on slide **10**, preview the project and retake the quiz (this time getting the first question wrong to see the edited feedback caption).

11. Save and close the project.

Knowledge Checks

During this module you learned how to insert graded questions. You can also add **Pretest** questions (questions with right and wrong answers that can be worth points but are not graded) and **Knowledge Checks**.

Knowledge Check slides behave like any other question slide with a few notable exceptions. As mentioned above, Pretest questions can be worth points; Knowledge Check questions cannot. There is also significantly more you, as a developer, can do with Knowledge Check slides. Compare the two images below. The image at the left shows the available Pretest question Actions (via the Properties Inspector). The second image shows Knowledge Check Actions. Knowledge Check slides are often used for review purposes. You can use the available Actions to reinforce learning.

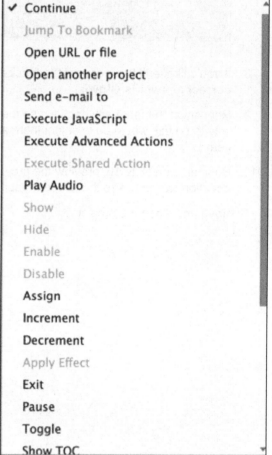

Guided Activity 76: Compare Submit All to Submit Buttons

1. Open **KnowledgeMe** from the **Captivate2019Data** folder.

2. Go to slide **11**.

   When you set up the Quiz Preferences for the last project, I mentioned Submit versus Submit All (page 202). This project is using the Submit All option. Let's see how Submit All compares with Submit.

3. Test the Submit All button.

   ☐ beginning on slide **10**, preview the project and take the quiz.

   ☐ prior to answering a question, click the **Submit All** button

An alert appears telling you that you first need to answer **all** of the questions.

☐ click the **OK** button

☐ answer the first question (it does not matter if you get the question right or wrong)

☐ click the **Submit All** button

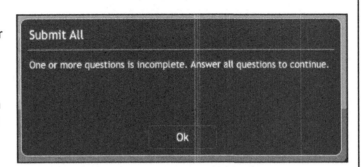

Because you still have not answered all of the questions, you'll get the **Submit All** alert.

☐ click the **OK** button and then click the **Next** button

This is the last question in the quiz. After answering this question, it is appropriate to click Submit All. However, you're going to "forget" to click Submit All and click Next instead. In a quiz with a standard Submit button, clicking Next does not submit the answer and you'd get the question wrong (even if you answered the question correctly).

☐ answer the Question and then click the **Next** button

This time you'll be prompted to Submit All of the questions.

☐ click the **Submit All Answers** button

You then move on to the Quiz results side.

4. Close the preview.

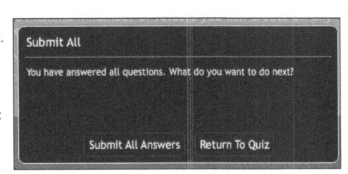

Guided Activity 77: Insert a Knowledge Check

1. Ensure that the **KnowledgeMe** project is open.

2. Insert a Knowledge Check Slide.

   ❑ on the **Filmstrip**, select slide **2**

   ❑ choose **Quiz > Knowledge Check Slide**

   As with standard quiz questions, the Insert Questions dialog box opens.

   ❑ select **Multiple Choice**

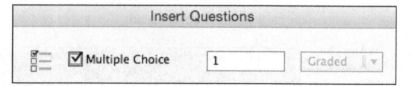

   Notice that the Graded drop-down menu is disabled because Knowledge Checks are not scored.

   ❑ click the **OK** button

   The Knowledge Check slide appears on the Filmstrip just like any other slide. However, notice that the slide includes a graduation cap icon not seen with the other slide types.

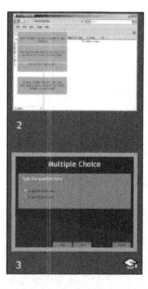

Knowledge Check Confidence Check

1. Edit the Knowledge Check Slide as follows:

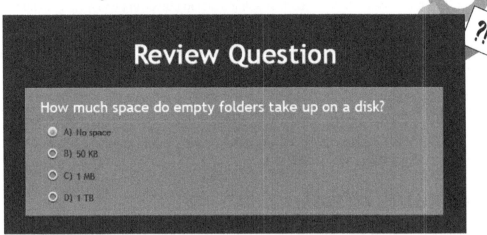

2. Insert a second Knowledge Check Slide after the first one that looks like this:

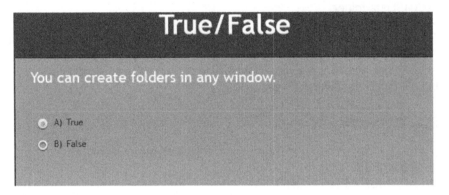

3. Preview the project.

4. When you get to the first Knowledge Check slide, answer the first question incorrectly and click **Submit**.

   You'll be prompted to Try again.

5. Answer the question correctly and click **Submit**.

6. Answer the next question correctly and click **Submit** to begin the main part of the course.

7. Work through the lesson and take the quiz at the end.

   The Quiz Results slide shows you the results of the quiz, but the Knowledge Check results are not included.

8. Close the preview.

9. Save and close the project.

Gift Files

To add question slides to a Captivate project, you can visit the Quiz menu and choose Question Slide. You'll be presented with the Insert Questions dialog box giving you access to several types of questions you can add including Multiple Choice, True/False, and Matching. Once the questions have been added to your project, the next step is to edit the questions and answers. If you need to add a large number of question slides to a project, you will need an incredible amount of time to create the quiz.

There is a better way to go, especially if the person creating the quiz does not have or use Adobe Captivate... **GIFT** or **CSV** files. GIFT stands for General Import Format Technology. You can create a GIFT file in plain text using a simple word processor (like Notepad or TextEdit) and then import the file into Adobe Captivate. CSV stands for comma separated value commonly used with spreadsheet programs click Microsoft Excel.

Guided Activity 78: Review a GIFT File

1. Minimize/Hide Adobe Captivate.

2. Using either Notepad (Windows) or TextEdit (Mac), open **GiftMe** from the Captivate2019Data folder.

   The GIFT file is a simple text file containing one multiple choice question. The syntax is simple. The Question Title goes between the double set of colons. Next comes the question itself. The answers are within the {}. The correct answer is preceded by an equal sign (=); the incorrect answers are preceded by a tilde (~).

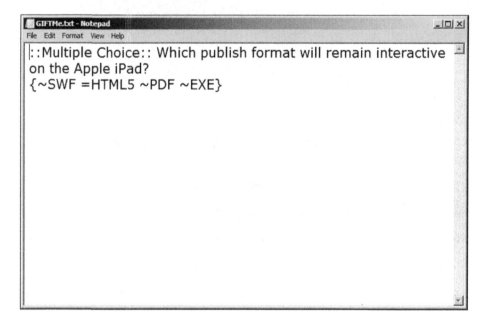

3. Close the GiftMe file (do not save any changes if prompted).

Guided Activity 79: Import a GIFT File into a Project

1. Open **PoolMe** from the **Captivate2019Data** folder.

   The project contains a 19-question quiz made up of True/False and Multiple Choice questions. You will soon create three Question Pools that contribute to a random quiz. But first, let's add a new question slide using the GIFT file you just reviewed.

2. Import a GIFT file.

   ❑ ensure slide **1** is selected

   ❑ choose **Quiz > Import GIFT Format File**

   ❑ from the **Captivate2019Data** folder, open **GiftMe.txt**

   A multiple choice question is added to the project after the selected slide 1.

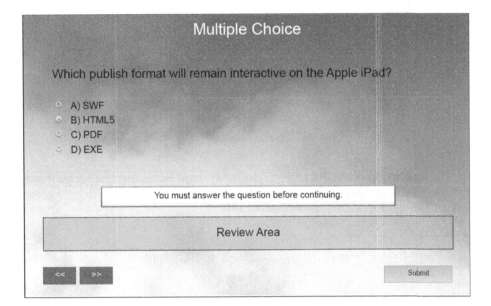

Question Pools

Creating a random quiz begins with Question Pools. Each Captivate project contains a single Question Pool (named Pool1). You can create as many pools as you need. The more Question Pools you have and the more question slides you have in each pool, the more random your quiz will be.

Guided Activity 80: Create Question Pools

1. Ensure that the **PoolMe** project is still open.

2. Display the Question Pool Manager.

   ❏ choose **Quiz > Question Pool Manager**

   The Question Pool Manager dialog box opens. By default, there is one pool named **Pool1**.

3. Create a Question Pool.

   ❏ click the plus sign above the existing Pool1 Question Pool

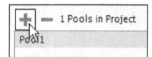

There are now two Pools in the project. Currently, both Pools are empty, but not for long. And although you can give a pool any name you like (as long as you don't use spaces in the pool's name), the default name works perfectly.

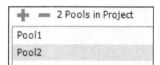

   ❏ click the **Close** button

Instead of seeing a slide in the middle of the screen, you see an Empty Question Pool. When you add question slides to the pools, this area of the Captivate window fills with content.

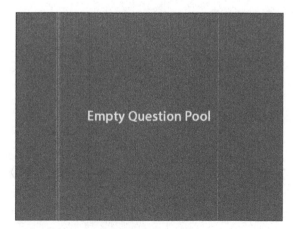

Question Pools Confidence Check

1. Ensure that the **PoolMe** project is still open.

2. Choose **Window > Question Pool**.

   The Question Pool panel appears at the bottom of the Captivate window (next to the Timeline). This area populates with questions as you move the project's question slides to the question pools.

3. The project's two Question Pools are empty (you can view each of your two pools via the drop-down menu at the right of the Question Pool panel).

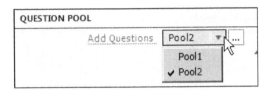

4. At the far right of Question Pool panel, click Question Pool Manager (the three dots).

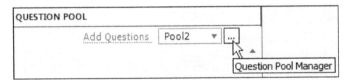

5. Create a third Question Pool (click the **Close** button when finished).

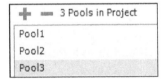

6. Save your work.

Guided Activity 81: Move Questions to Pools

1. Ensure that the **PoolMe** project is still open.

2. Move a Question Slide to a Question Pool.

   ☐ on the Filmstrip, right-click slide **2** and choose **Move Question to > Pool1**

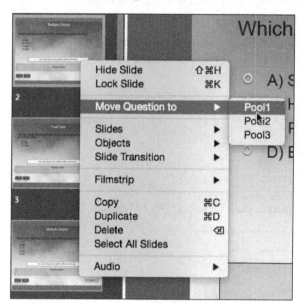

The slide disappears from the Filmstrip. No worries! It's safe and sound in the Pool1 pool (which you will see soon enough on the Question Pools panel).

3. Move another Question Slide to a Question Pool.

   ☐ on the Filmstrip, right-click slide **2** and choose **Move Question to > Pool2**

4. View Question Slides in their respective Pools.

   ☐ on the Question Pool panel, select **Pool1** and then **Pool2** from the drop-down menu to view the single Question Slide in each Pool

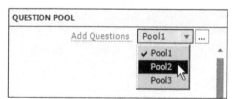

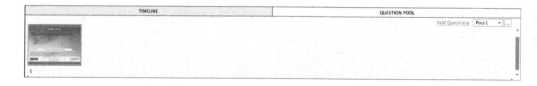

Moving Questions Confidence Check

On the Filmstrip, slides 2 through 19 are all Question Slides and need to be added to the Question Pools. (Slides 1 and 20 are not Question Slides, so you will not be able to accidentally add them to any of the Pools.)

1. Beginning with slide 2 on the Filmstrip, add the Question Slides to the Question Pools randomly or as you see fit.

2. Display the **Question Pool Manager** (Quiz menu).

3. Select each of the Pools one by one and, from the information that appears at the left of the Question Pool Manager, notice how many questions are in each pool.

   If you would like to move a question from one pool to another, return to the Question Pool panel, right-click any question, and choose **Move Question to**.

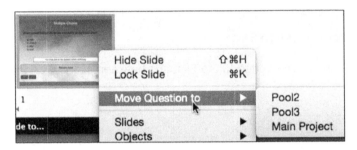

4. Close the Question Pools Manager.

5. Save your work.

Random Question Slides

Up to this point you've created Question Pools and moved all of the questions in the project to the pools. In the process, you've removed all of the slides from the Filmstrip. So how will Captivate serve up a random quiz to your learners if there aren't any questions on the Filmstrip to publish? The answer lies in a bit of brilliance devised by Adobe: Random Question Slides. You'll add some Random Question Slides to the Filmstrip to serve as proxies for the missing question slides. Because you can link each Random Question Slide to a Question Pool, a question is randomly selected from the pool and presented to the learner during the quiz.

Guided Activity 82: Insert Random Question Slides

1. Ensure that the **PoolMe** project is still open.

2. Insert a Random Question Slide.

   ☐ on the Filmstrip, select slide **1**

   ☐ choose **Quiz > Random Question Slide**

   A Random Question slide has been added to the Filmstrip between slides **1** and **3**.

3. Link the Random Question Slide to a Question Pool.

   ☐ on the **Quiz Inspector**, (the Quiz Inspector is at the right of the Captivate window, next to the Properties Inspector), select from any of the pools from the **Question Pool** drop-down menu

   ☐ change the **Points** to **1**

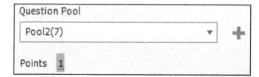

Random Questions Confidence Check

1. Insert four more Random Question Slides.

   Ensure that the Points are set to 1 for each of the slides and that they are linked to any of the Question Pools you like.

   You should now have **five Random Question Slides** in your project.

2. Preview the project and take the quiz. Pay particular attention to the questions that appear.

3. Close the preview.

4. Preview the project and take the quiz again.

   Because you used Random Question Slides that pull questions from three different Pools, the questions you see should be at least a little different from the first time you took the quiz.

5. Close the preview.

6. Save and close the project.

Notes

Module 13: Publishing

In This Module You Will Learn About:

- Skins, page 222
- Table of Contents, page 226
- Preloaders, page 230
- Publishing, page 233

And You Will Learn To:

- Apply a Skin, page 222
- Edit, Save, and Delete a Skin, page 223
- Name Slides, page 226
- Check Publish Settings and Add a Loading Screen, page 230
- Publish as SWF and PDF, page 233
- Run the HTML5 Tracker, page 239
- Publish as HTML5, page 240

Skins

Skins perform much the same function for a project as your clothes perform for you. Bored? Bummed? Perhaps something simple like changing your clothes would be enough to change your attitude. Consider some of the top websites in the world. During the holiday season, sites like amazon.com and google.com change the whole attitude of their site just by changing the "skin" used on their sites to reflect the season. The sites themselves don't change; just the outer skin changes.

You are about to learn how easy it is to change the skin used by your project. And you will learn that Skins can be customized to suit your taste—you can select from several playbars, buttons, and color schemes.

Guided Activity 83: Apply a Skin

1. Open **FinishMe** from the **Captivate2019Data** folder.

2. Preview the project and notice that there is a playbar at the bottom of the lesson window. The playbar is just one component of a Skin.

3. Close the preview.

4. Apply a skin to the project.

   ☐ choose **Project > Skin Editor**

   ☐ from the top of the Skin Editor, select the **Playback Control** button

   ☐ from the **Skin** drop-down menu, choose **Pearls**

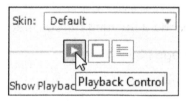

5. Preview the Project.

   Notice the Pearls skin has been applied to the lesson.

6. Close the preview.

Guided Activity 84: Edit, Save, and Delete a Skin

1. Ensure that the **FinishMe** project is still open.

2. Remove an unnecessary control from the playbar.

   ❏ with the Skin Editor still open (Project or Window menu), ensure **Pearls** is selected from the **Skin** drop-down menu

   ❏ from the lower left of the Skin Editor window, remove the check mark from **Closed Captioning**

   Because this project does not have any closed captions, the Closed Captioning option is not needed. (Closed Captions are important; they are covered in *Adobe Captivate 2019: Beyond the Essentials*.)

3. Save the modifications to the skin as a new skin.

   ❏ click the **Save As** button

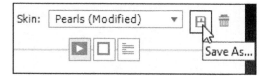

   The Save As dialog box opens.

   ❏ change the name to **Pearls_NoCC**

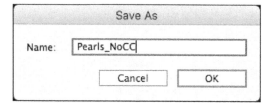

   ❏ click the **OK** button

4. Apply a different skin.

   ❏ from the Skin drop-down menu, choose **DarkChocolate**

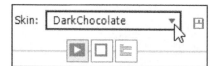

Notice on the preview that the color of your playbar changes to reflect the new skin.

5. Reapply the edited Pearls skin.

   ☐ from the Skin drop-down menu, choose **Pearls_NoCC**

   The preview returns to your selected skin.

6. Delete a skin.

   ☐ ensure that **Pearls_NoCC** is the selected Skin

   ☐ click the **Delete** button

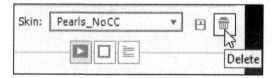

Project Information Confidence Check

1. Still working in the **FinishMe** project, spend a few moments applying some of the other skins to your project.

2. After you have settled on your favorite skin, preview the project to ensure the skin still meets with your approval.

3. Edit the skin so that it does not use the Closed Captioning option.

4. Save the edited skin with a name that reflects the missing Closed Captioning (such as **name_NoCC**).

5. Close the Skin Editor window.

6. Choose **File > Project Info**.

7. Fill in the information with your personal information (some of the information that you type here will appear on a Table of Contents panel that you are about to create).

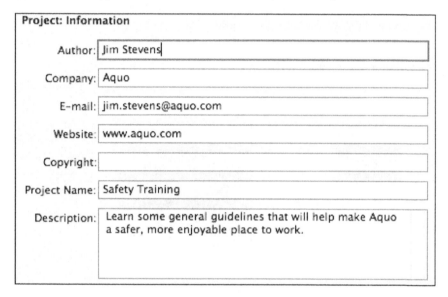

Project: Information	
Author:	Jim Stevens
Company:	Aquo
E-mail:	jim.stevens@aquo.com
Website:	www.aquo.com
Copyright:	
Project Name:	Safety Training
Description:	Learn some general guidelines that will help make Aquo a safer, more enjoyable place to work.

8. Click the **OK** button.

9. Save your work.

NOTES

Table of Contents

You can create a Table of Contents (TOC) that serves as a navigation aid for your learners. Creating the TOC is as simple as selecting **Show TOC** on the TOC tab of the Skin Editor. A TOC typically appears at the right or left of the lesson, making the lesson wider by a minimum of 250 pixels (something to consider if your lesson is already pretty wide).

Guided Activity 85: Name Slides

1. Ensure that the **FinishMe** project is still open.

2. Name the slide.

   ☐ select slide **1**

   ☐ at the top of the **Properties** Inspector, name the slide **Introduction Video**

On the Filmstrip, the name you just typed appears on the slide's thumbnail. The name will also appear on the TOC you will create shortly.

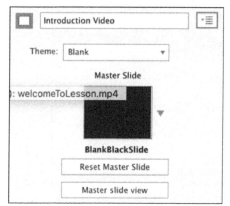

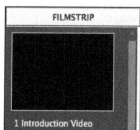

   ☐ select slide **2**

   ☐ at the top of the **Properties** Inspector, name the slide **Jim Stevens' Welcome**

Naming Slides Confidence Check

Still working in the FinishMe project, give the following slides names as indicated (the slides that don't get names will not appear on the TOC):

   ☐ Slide 3: **Lesson Overview**

   ☐ Slide 4: **Personal Protective Equipment**

   ☐ Slide 5: **Gloves**

   ☐ Slide 6: **Shirts and Coats**

   ☐ Slide 7: **Hard Hats**

   ☐ Slide 8: **Work Boots**

   ☐ Slide 9: **Safety Goggles**

   ☐ Slide 10: **Quiz**

   ☐ Slide 14: **Replay**

Guided Activity 86: Create a TOC

1. Ensure that the **FinishMe** project is still open.

2. Show the TOC.

   ☐ **Project > Table of Contents**

   The Skin Editor opens again, but this time you are on the Table of Contents tab.

   ☐ from the left side of the Skin Editor, select **Show TOC**

   A TOC is added to the left of the lesson. Next you reset the TOC to the names you gave most of the slides appear on the TOC.

3. Reset the TOC.

   ☐ at the bottom left of the Skin Editor, click **Reset TOC**

   The slide names are added to the TOC.

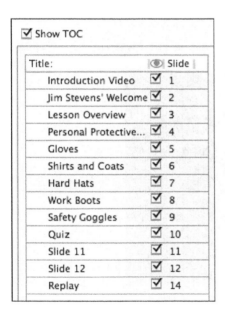

4. Remove select slides from the TOC.

   ☐ on the TOC, remove the check mark from slides **11** and **12**

Quiz	☑	10
Slide 11	☐	11
Slide 12	☐	12
Replay	☑	14

   The two slides are removed from the TOC.

NOTES

TOC Confidence Check

1. Still working in the FinishMe project, click the **Settings** button at the bottom of the TOC.

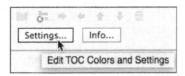

2. From the **Runtime Options** area, remove the check mark from **Show Topic Duration**.

3. From the **Runtime Options** area, select **Status Flag**.

4. Ensure the remaining Runtime Options match the image below and then click the **OK** button.

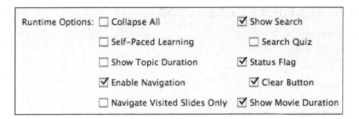

5. Preview the project and notice that the lesson now includes a TOC.

6. As you move through the lesson, check marks are automatically added to the TOC (thanks to the Status Flag option you just selected). *Nice!*

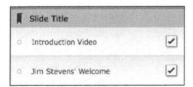

7. Close the preview.

8. Open the Table of Contents window (if necessary) and from the bottom of the window, click the **Info** button.

9. You added project information earlier (page 225), but the information isn't here. Or is it? Click the **Project Information** button.

   The fields on the TOC information dialog box populate using the project information you added earlier.

10. In the **Photo** area, click the yellow **Browse** folder.

    The Select Image from Library dialog box opens.

11. Click the **Import** button.

12. From the **Captivate2019Data** > **images** folder, open **JimStevens**.

    You should be back in the main TOC Information dialog box. The name of the image you opened displays in the **Photo** area.

13. In the Title area, type **Aquo Safety Training**

14. In the Designation field, type **Facilities Safety Director**

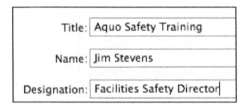

15. Click the **OK** button to close the TOC Information dialog box.

16. Notice in the Preview window at the right that the information and photo appear on the TOC.

17. At the bottom left of the TOC, click the **Settings** button

18. From the **Theme** area, click the **Background** color box and select any color you like

19. Make any other color changes that you like to any of the items and click the **OK** button

20. On the Skin Editor, select the **Playback Control** tab (it's the first tab).

21. From the **Theme** area, select **Playback Colors**.

22. Change the colors of the Playback controls as you see fit.

23. Close the Skin Editor window and save your work.

Preloaders

If your learner is using a slow Internet connection and your lesson is large (over 10-15 megabytes), it could take a significant amount of time for the lesson to begin playing on the learner's computer or mobile device. Because most people do not wait for more than a few seconds for something to happen on their device before giving up, a loading screen—an image or message that appears during those first seconds while the initial part of the published lesson is downloading—is critical.

Guided Activity 87: Check Publish Settings and Add a Loading Screen

1. Ensure that the **FinishMe** project is still open.

2. Confirm the Publish Settings.

   ☐ choose **File > Publish Settings**

   ☐ ensure that your Settings match the picture below (all are Captivate defaults)

Project: Publish Settings

Frames Per Second: `30`

Language `English...  ▼`

☐ Publish Adobe Connect metadata.

☑ Include Mouse

☑ Enable Accessibility

☐ Restrict keyboard tabbing to slide items only

☑ Hide selection rectangle for slide items in HTML5

☑ Include Audio

☑ Publish Audio as Mono

☑ Play tap audio for recorded typing

Externalize Resources: ☐ Skin

☐ Widgets

☐ FMR SWF

☐ Animations

Most of the Publish Settings are self-explanatory. However, I'll explain some of the more important options below. (If you want to know more about the options, click the Help link at the bottom of the dialog box.)

Frames Per Second is a measure of how smoothly your published lesson plays. Remember when you were a kid and you made your very own cartoon by drawing a simple stick figure on several pieces of paper? The more pieces of paper you had and the more poses you added to your cartoon character, the more realistic the cartoon looked when you fanned through all of the pieces of paper. The same idea holds true with Frames Per Second. The more frames you have, the smoother your lesson will be. The Captivate default is 30 Frames Per Second, which is plenty. I don't suggest lowering or raising the Frames Per Second unless you are specifically instructed to do so by someone on your team who's in the know. (I've never changed the Frames Per Second in any of my projects.)

Externalize Resources. One goal when publishing your content is to keep the number of published files to a minimum, making file management and uploads to web servers easy. By default, resources such as Skins and Animations are embedded within the published lesson file, resulting in a larger SWF. Unless your SWFs are huge, consider leaving the options as shown on the previous page.

3. Add a loading screen.

   ❏ from the **Project category** at the left, select **Start and End**

   ❏ select **Preloader**

   ❏ click the **Browse** button to the right of Preloader

   You should automatically be browsing the Preloaders folder that comes with Captivate (if not, you can manually browse to the folder via **Gallery > Preloaders**). The Preloader is what the learners see while they are waiting for the lesson to begin playing.

   ❏ navigate to the **Captivate2019Data > images** folder

   ❏ open **Aquo.gif**

4. Set a Preloader %.

   ❏ change the **Preloader %** to **50**

☑ Preloader:		
nlogic/Desktop/Captivate2019Data/images/AQUO.gif		Browse...
Preloader %:	50	

   The Preloader % is the percentage of the published Captivate SWF file that must be downloaded to the learner's device before the lesson begins to play. Setting the percentage to 50 percent is pretty standard. I wouldn't suggest going too low (which results in a sputtering playback) or too high (which takes too long for the lesson to begin).

5. Set the project fade options.

   ❏ if necessary, select **Fade In on the First slide**

   ❏ from the **Action** drop-down menu in the **Project End Options** area, ensure **Stop project** is selected

   ❏ if necessary, deselect **Fade Out on the Last slide**

Fading in on the first slide is a nice effect. However, I've discovered that fading out on the last slide doesn't offer nearly the same impact. In fact, if you leave it selected, you may find that it causes other problems with items on your Timeline that also fade in and/or fade out with objects that pause the slide action. As for the Actions area, I prefer the Stop Project action. When the lesson is finished, it will stop. The learner can then elect to rewind the lesson or close the lesson.

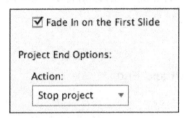

☐ click the **OK** button

6. Save your work.

Publishing

Publishing in Captivate takes your source content and outputs it into a format that can be consumed (viewed) by the learner via a web browser. One common way to publish a Captivate project is as a Flash SWF, a reasonable option because SWF files can be used by many of the world's desktop and laptop computers. Your learners do **not** need Captivate installed on their computer to access your published content, but they do need a web browser (they're typically free) that supports Flash, a device that supports Flash (these days those devices are typically limited to desktop and laptop computers, not mobile devices), and the free Adobe Flash Player.

While Flash was once the worldwide multimedia standard, that is no longer the case. Thanks to several well-publicized Flash security vulnerabilities and other "issues," many organizations now block Flash content. Learners using mobile devices, such as smart phones and tablets (that's millions of learners), cannot open anything containing Flash content. Many of today's browsers (such as Google Chrome) block Flash by default. And given that Adobe announced that Flash would no longer be supported by the end of 2020, publishing SWFs means your content will likely become obsolete in the near term.

As an alternative to publishing SWFs, you can publish your content as HTML5. Lessons published as HTML5 play on any computer or mobile device that supports HTML5, including most mobile devices.

I know what you're thinking: if Flash is getting sunset by Adobe in 2020, why publish as SWF at all? It's true that some browsers and most mobile devices cannot open SWFs. However, older systems and browsers love SWFs and cannot open HTML5.

Should you publish as HTML5? SWF? Both? None of the above? You can publish as a PDF but PDFs include Flash content so they are not appropriate for devices that don't support Flash. This whole publishing thing is a quandary that many eLearning developers are facing. My personal feeling is that publishing as HTML5 these days is far safer than publishing as SWF or PDF, but there are many people who disagree with me. If you are a freelance developer, meet with your client and discuss the expected hardware/software restrictions for the learners. If you work for an organization with IT support, I'd suggest discussing the pros and cons of SWF and HTML5 sooner rather than later and planning your project creation and publishing strategy accordingly.

Guided Activity 88: Publish as SWF and PDF

1. Ensure that the **FinishMe** project is still open.

2. Specify a Publish format and Project Title.

   ☐ choose **File > Publish**

   The Publish dialog box opens.

   ☐ from **Publish as** drop-down menu, ensure **HTML5/SWF** is selected

   ☐ if necessary, change the **Project Title** to **AquoSafety**

   The Project Title ends up being the physical name of the files you publish. Because your published files are likely to be stored on a web server, never use spaces in Project Titles.

3. Select the Output Format.

☐ from the **Output Format** area, select **SWF** and, if necessary, **deselect HTML5**

The SWF button should be darker, indicating it is your selected publish format. The HTML5 should be lighter. Although you can publish both SWF and HTML5 at the same time, you'll be publishing them separately and then reviewing the files that are physically published.

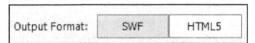

4. Select a Location for the published assets.

☐ at the right of the **Location** field, click the **yellow browse** folder

☐ navigate to **Captivate2019Data** folder

☐ open the **published_projects** folder

☐ click the **Select Folder** button (**Choose** on the Mac)

☐ back in the Publish dialog box, from beneath the **Location** area, select **Publish To Folder**

The **Publish to Folder** option creates a folder inside the **published_projects** folder called **AquoSafety**. There will be occasions when you do not want to create a new folder when publishing—a decision you make on a project-by-project basis.

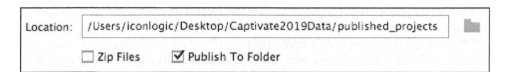

You would typically select **Zip Files** only if you intend to upload your project to an Learning Management System. (You learn how to set up a project to work with LMSs in my *Adobe Captivate 2019: Beyond the Essentials (Second Edition)* book.)

The Fullscreen option causes your published lesson to take over the learner's entire screen; something that most learners do not appreciate.

5. Export a PDF and select the Flash Player Version.

☐ from the **Output Format** area, select **Export PDF**

The PDF you create includes all of the lesson's animations, audio, and interactivity. Any learner who has Adobe Reader 9 or newer and the latest Adobe Flash Player can work with your content.

☐ from the **Flash Player Version** drop-down menu, select **Flash Player 10**

At the time that this book was written, Flash Player 11 was the newest version of the Flash Player available from within Captivate. However, if you select a Flash Player version that's too new, learners who have an older version of the Flash Player would be unable to watch your published lesson. By selecting Flash Player 10, or even 10.2, which is more widely used than version 11, it's likely that most learners will be able to view your content.

❏ ensure **Force re-publish on all slides** is selected

With **Force re-publish on all slides**, Captivate publishes everything on all slides, even if a slide has not changed since the last time you published. When you deselect this option, the publish process is quicker. However, I've found that every once in a while edited slides do not appear edited in the published version of the lesson. Given that, I always Force republish.

❏ select **Scalable HTML content**

With this option selected, the lesson window will resize to match the size of the learner's display.

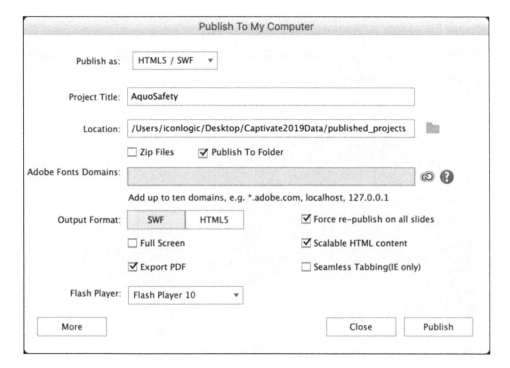

6. Publish the lesson.

   ❏ click the **Publish** button

Because you selected Export PDF, you are presented with an alert dialog box letting you know that learners need the free Adobe Reader 9 or newer to work with the Flash content within the PDF.

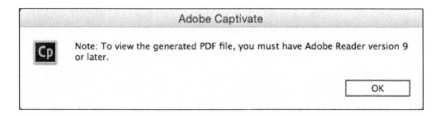

❏ click the **OK** button

Next you are prompted to view the output.

☐ click the **No** button (you'll be previewing both the SWF and the PDF published content in just a moment)

7. Review the assets published to the Publish folder.

☐ minimize (Hide) Captivate and navigate to **Captivate2019Data > published_projects**

☐ open the **AquoSafety** folder

The Publish process has produced several files.

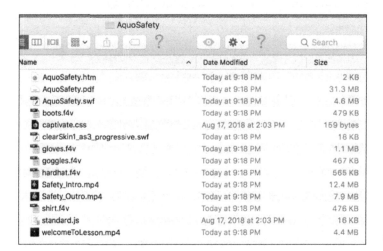

There's an SWF, an HTML file, videos, and a PDF. The SWF contains the lesson, and it's the file learners will be interacting with via a web browser. There is also a JavaScript file (standard.js) and a CSS file (captivate.css). The role of the JS and CSS files is to ensure that the SWF appears and plays without being blocked by the web browser. And the HTML file is the **start page for the lesson**. Once the HTML file is opened by a web browser, code within the HTML page loads into the browser and immediately looks for the JavaScript and CSS files. Assuming the files are located, the SWF file plays within the web browser. *The SWF, HTML, JS, and CSS files should always be kept together. Lose any one of the files, and the lesson will not play.* The PDF is a standalone asset that only needs Adobe Reader and Adobe Flash Player.

8. View the published SWF.

❐ from within the **AquoSafety** folder, open **AquoSafety.htm**

The HTML file loads the SWF into your default web browser, and the lesson opens. Keep in mind that learners who attempt to work with an SWF must be on a device that supports SWFs, and they must have a web browser.

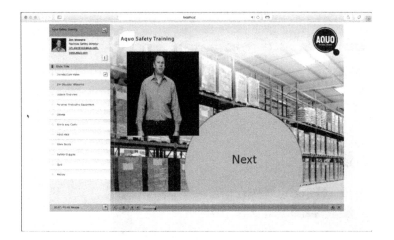

Note: Did you have trouble with video playback? There are several reasons that the lesson might not play as expected on your computer. It's possible you need to upload the published assets to your web server and test from there (often times your browser blocks assets/features—such as videos—when you test them locally). You might also need to update your version of the Flash Player (it's free and can be downloaded from Adobe's website). It's also possible that SWFs are blocked by your organization or your browser. In that case, SWFs either won't play at all (or not correctly) and neither will the PDF. No worries, because it's likely that the HTML5 version of the project will play just fine on your computer, you'll be able to see your published lesson in action soon (You'll be publishing HTML5 on page 240.)

❐ close the browser window

9. View the published PDF.

❏ from within the AquoSafety folder, open **AquoSafety.pdf**

The lesson opens just as it did when you opened the HTML file. However, this version of the lesson is running within Adobe Reader or Adobe Acrobat (depending upon what is installed on your computer). The lesson isn't using a web browser but includes all of the media (audio, videos, and interactivity).

Note: As mentioned earlier, if your organization, browser, or computer is blocking Flash content, it's likely that the PDF isn't working correctly because it contains Flash. If you see a **blank white page** instead of the lesson, you're being blocked and there isn't much you can do about it beyond attempting to update your Flash Player and/or Adobe Reader.

10. Close the PDF and return to the Captivate project.

Guided Activity 89: Run the HTML5 Tracker

1. Ensure that the **FinishMe** project is still open.

2. Test the lesson to see if it is appropriate for HTML5.

   ☐ choose **Project > HTML5 Tracker**

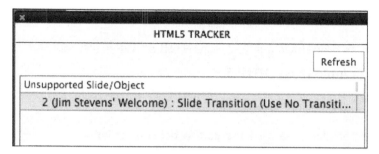

   Although this lesson works fine on a device that supports Flash (SWFs), HTML5 has limitations. Fortunately, there's only one issue found with the current project: the slide transition.

3. Close the HTML5 Tracker window.

4. Remove the slide transition.

   ☐ select slide **2**

   ☐ on the Timing Inspector, change the Transition to **No Transition**

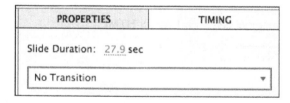

5. Re-test the lesson to see if it is appropriate for HTML5.

   ☐ choose **Project > HTML5 Tracker**

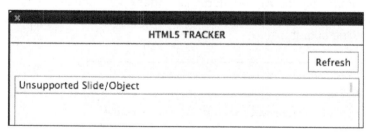

   Your project does not have any HTML5-compliance issues so the HTML Tracker is wonderfully empty.

6. Close the HTML5 Tracker window.

Guided Activity 90: Publish as HTML5

1. Ensure that the **FinishMe** project is still open.

2. Publish as HTML5.

   ☐ choose **File > Publish**

   The Publish dialog box opens.

   ☐ from the **Publish as** drop-down menu, ensure **HTML5/SWF** is still selected
   ☐ change the Title to **AquoSafety_HTML5**

3. Select a Location for the published assets.

   ☐ at the right of the Location area, click the **yellow browse** folder
   ☐ navigate to **Captivate2019Data** folder
   ☐ open the **published_projects** folder and then click the **Select Folder** button (**Choose** on the Mac)

4. Select HTML5 as the Output Format.

   ☐ from the **Output Format** area, deselect **SWF** and select **HTML5**

5. Publish the HTML5 output.

   ☐ click the **Publish** button

   During the Publishing process, the **Adobe Media Encoder** opens and automatically converts the lesson's videos for use as HTML5. Once the Publish process completes, you are prompted to view the output.

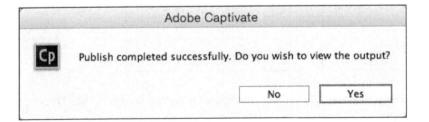

   ☐ click the **No** button (you'll be viewing the content in just a moment)

---

6. Review the HTML5 published assets.

  ☐ minimize (Hide) Captivate

  ☐ navigate to **Captivate2019Data > published_projects** and open the **AquoSafety_HTML5** folder

There are far more assets with the HTML5 output than what resulted from publishing as a SWF. These assets are dependent on each other so everything must be kept together when posted to a web server.

Name	^	Date Modified
▶ ar		Today at 9:47 PM
▶ assets		Today at 9:47 PM
▶ callees		Today at 9:47 PM
▶ dr		Today at 9:47 PM
⦿ goodbye.html		Aug 17, 2018 at 2:03 PM
⦿ index.html		Today at 9:49 PM
project.txt		Today at 9:49 PM
▶ vr		Today at 9:49 PM

  ☐ open **index** with your web browser to view the lesson

The lesson opens in your browser and plays as expected. And because it's HTML5, it will work as it does now when opened with mobile devices such as the smart phones or tablets.

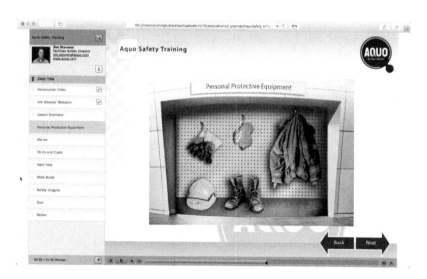

7. Close the browser.

8. Return to the FinishMe Captivate project and save and close the project.

And a hearty congratulations are in order... you have completed this book. There's much more to Captivate of course (see the next page), but you should now feel comfortable creating new projects and recording screen actions. You should be able to add standard objects such as click boxes, buttons, text entry boxes, images, characters, videos, and animations. And you should feel comfortable in your ability to not only Publish your content but create output files appropriate for the kind of device you expect your learners to be using.

Want to Learn More About Adobe Captivate?

By completing the lessons in this book, you have learned the essential skills that enable you to immediately create effective soft skills learning, demonstrations, and simulations in Adobe Captivate.

If you'd like to go beyond the basics and learn even more about Captivate, consider *Adobe Captivate 2019: Beyond the Essentials*.

Topics covered in *Adobe Captivate 2019: Beyond the Essentials* include, but are not limited to, the following:

- ❏ Interactive Videos
- ❏ Virtual Reality Projects
- ❏ Project Templates & Custom Themes
- ❏ Master Slides
- ❏ Custom Object Styles
- ❏ Branching Scenarios
- ❏ Responsive Projects
- ❏ Widgets
- ❏ Variables
- ❏ Advanced Actions
- ❏ LMS Integration

You can learn more about IconLogic's books, live online Captivate training and mentoring, certification, and full eLearning development support at **www.iconlogic.com**.

Index

NOTES

NOTES

NOTES

Made in the USA
Columbia, SC
16 May 2020

Made in the USA
Columbia, SC
16 May 2020